COSTUME EN FACE

A PRIMER OF DARKNESS FOR YOUNG BOYS AND GIRLS

TATSUMI HIJIKATA

NOTEBOOK WRITTEN BY MOE YAMAMOTO
AND TRANSLATED FROM THE JAPANESE BY
SAWAKO NAKAYASU

EMERGENCY PLAYSCRIPTS
UGLY DUCKLING PRESSE
BROOKLYN, NY

COSTUME EN FACE:
A PRIMER OF DARKNESS
FOR YOUNG BOYS AND GIRLS

ENGLISH TRANSLATION
COPYRIGHT SAWAKO NAKAYASU, 2015, 2018

COSTUME EN FACE (ORIGINAL NOTEBOOK)
COPYRIGHT MOE YAMAMOTO, 1976

ESSAY: *SHŌMEN NO ISHŌ* (COSTUME
EN FACE): *BUTOH IN 1976*
COPYRIGHT TAKASHI MORISHITA, 2010

EMERGENCY PLAYSCRIPTS #4

ISBN 978-1-937027-53-7

SERIES EDITOR
YELENA GLUZMAN

SERIES PUBLISHERS
THE BROS. LUMIÈRE

FIRST EDITION, 2015
SECOND PRINTING, 2018
UGLY DUCKLING PRESSE
232 THIRD STREET, E-303
BROOKLYN, NY 11215
>UGLYDUCKLINGPRESSE.ORG<

FUNDED IN PART BY
THE NATIONAL ENDOWMENT
FOR THE ARTS
THE FOUNDATION FOR
CONTEMPORARY ARTS
KEIO UNIVERSITY ART CENTER

DISTRIBUTED IN THE US BY
SMALL PRESS DISTRIBUTION
>SPDBOOKS.ORG<

DISTRIBUTED IN THE UK BY
INPRESS BOOKS
>INPRESSBOOKS.CO.UK<

DISTRIBUTED IN CANADA
VIA COACH HOUSE BOOKS BY
RAINCOAST BOOKS
>RAINCOAST.COM<

PRINTED IN THE USA

COSTUME EN FACE

A PRIMER OF DARKNESS
FOR YOUNG BOYS AND GIRLS

TATSUMI HIJIKATA

NOTEBOOK WRITTEN BY MOE YAMAMOTO

TRANSLATED FROM THE JAPANESE BY
SAWAKO NAKAYASU

GRAPHIC TRANSLATION & BOOK DESIGN BY
STEVEN CHODORIWSKY

CONTENTS

ILLUSTRATIONS   7

INTRODUCTION
    BY TAKASHI MORISHITA   9

TRANSLATOR'S NOTE   13

COSTUME EN FACE   14

SHŌMEN NO ISHŌ (COSTUME EN FACE): BUTOH IN 1976
    BY TAKASHI MORISHITA   128

EDITOR'S NOTE   139

INDEX   141

COLOPHON   143

ILLUSTRATIONS

1. COMB SCENE (くしの景)　11

2. SHAWL SCENE (ショールの景)　71

3. GOLDFISH SCENE (金魚の景)　114

4. GOLDFISH SCENE (金魚の景)　115

5. RHINOCEROS SCENE (犀の景)　127

DANCER IN DEPICTED SCENES: MOE YAMAMOTO. PHOTOGRAPHER UNKNOWN. ALL IMAGES COURTESY OF THE TATSUMI HIJIKATA ARCHIVE, KEIO UNIVERSITY ART CENTER, JAPAN.

INTRODUCTION

It makes sense to question whether this English translation of *Costume en Face*, a notation of Butoh dance, is Hijikata's work, or Moe Yamamoto's work.

Needless to say, this notebook is the documentation of words provided by Tatsumi Hijikata to Moe Yamamoto, in rehearsal preparation for a performance. Thus this document, which illustrates the structure of the Butoh work *Costume en Face*, could also be considered its script.

The words came from Hijikata, and yet the actual notation of these words are subject to a certain kind of arbitrariness, based on Moe Yamamoto's understanding and judgement. For each word in the notebook, there is attached a 'movement' invented by Hijikata. Words are a metaphor for 'movement.'

Regarding translation, the translator conducted an interview with Moe Yamamoto. Today, with the absence of Hijikata, the information we receive from Yamamoto is indispensable for the understanding of this 'notebook.'

But then again, even if Hijikata was around, it is doubtful whether he'd be able to provide suggestions or information that would be useful for the purposes of translation. It is not hard to imagine that it might even increase the confusion.

One interesting point that arose from the interview was the realization that this book does not represent a document which is closest to the actual performance (for which we have video documentation). In fact, there were some structural changes made to the piece in a rehearsal just before the performance. There remains a separate notebook that documents those changes.

This also relates to the above, but there is another fact, which is that Moe Yamamoto was not able to dance all of the parts that Hijikata had suggested. After all, it had only been two years that Moe Yamamoto had been under Hijikata's tutelage. It would be nearly impossible for him to have learned in two years how to perform perfectly all of the 'movements' created and suggested by Hijikata, and to dance it the way Hijikata had imagined it.

In any case, Tatsumi Hijikata created a work of Butoh dance called *Costume en Face*. It is only because of this method of creating dance, based on the notation of Butoh, that Moe Yamamoto was able to play the leading role, and that Hijikata was able to complete this work featuring Yamamoto.

The work of translating this notebook should lift a certain veil from what is known about Hijikata's Butoh. Let it shine a light upon Hijikata's working style and dance methods, the codification of 'movement' into language, the techniques of Butoh dance and performance. And, it should let us get a glimpse into 'the method of Butoh' which Hijikata himself was pursuing at the time.

Even then, the world that this work expresses still remains shrouded in mystery. It is not possible to learn this based on the few words of Moe Yamamoto. Moe Yamamoto himself was feverishly learning the dance, and remained unaware of the larger world that the piece inhabited. If we look for a hint from Hijikata, it may be something as simple as a goldfish in a fish bowl.

TAKASHI MORISHITA
DIRECTOR, TATSUMI HIJIKATA ARCHIVE, KEIO UNIVERSITY

TRANSLATOR'S NOTE

Often when I am faced with a difficult translation, that difficulty is met in silence if the writer of the original text is no longer among us. Creating this translation of *Costume en Face*, based on a notebook hand-written (and drawn) by Moe Yamamoto in 1976, then, was a unique situation: the writer of this notebook, Moe-san, is alive and well, and gave me the opportunity to meet with him and ask him questions. And yet the notebook itself was a document of transcription, a frantic scribbling of notes for a dance, one in which the dancer is focused on learning the movement and its textural qualities as they were dictated to him. Not only that, the mastermind of this coded work of art, Hijikata himself, is no longer with us, though in his stead, the generous and patient guardians of his archives at the Keio University Art Center (Morishita-san and Homma-san, to whom I am deeply grateful, and through whom I was able to meet with Moe-san), have guided and supported me in this deeply challenging task.

    Naturally there were illegible characters whose meaning was obscure even to the person who wrote them. The translation attempts to stay as close to the text as possible, and when a word could not be read, the absence is indicated by [...]. Japanese does not contain capitalization, and the convention used here is to employ capitals for proper names, names of movements and movement objects, and to mark the beginning of distinct phrases. In cases where terms specific to Japanese culture, mythology, or history are used, these are left in the original Japanese, and a brief explanation is provided in square brackets following the first instance of the word. The translation does not (and cannot) attempt to specify what particular phrases connoted: movements, movement sequences, instructions, qualities, or actual objects and costumes. In addition to Japanese sources, Hijikata drew from a great wealth of Western art, and showed his dancers many images in the rehearsal process. Thus a note like "Woman with spoon" refers to a specific painting by Goya, whereas artist names like Bellmer, Toyen, and Fautrier became code for specific movements inspired by their imagery. The book, however, is mute on definitions, and remains committed to interpretation and embodiment, not only of its original performers, but also of those of us trusted to edit, translate and design the book, and of the readers, dancers, scholars, poets and performance makers who will, in turn, take it up.

SAWAKO NAKAYASU

正面の衣裳

少年と少女のための闇の手本

土方巽

COSTUME EN FACE

A PRIMER OF DARKNESS FOR YOUNG BOYS AND GIRLS

TATSUMI HIJIKATA

3mの毛の固りの中のやく病神
フカンされた
毛の百鬼夜行
ガキ態の舞首

A　病んでいる表情　　1. 暗い顔
　　　　　　　　　　2. すすけた白い 〃
　　　　　　　　　　3. 拡大される 〃
　　　　　　　　　　4. ひき伸ばされた 〃

B　角度を付ける
　　3mもの毛の中で行なわれる

C　背景
　　湿け・臭い・すいび・闇
　　日のめをみられない‥‥夜のれい気

D　上よりフカンされるからさらに数が増えるだろう

注．抽象的なフンイキの中にのがさないように
　　部分の動きにかく闘

8

Yakubyōgami [god of pestilence] in a 3m clump of hair
        viewed from above
Hyakki Yagyō [night parade of one hundred demons] of hair
Maikubi [entity of dancing heads] in the form of Gaki [hungry ghost]

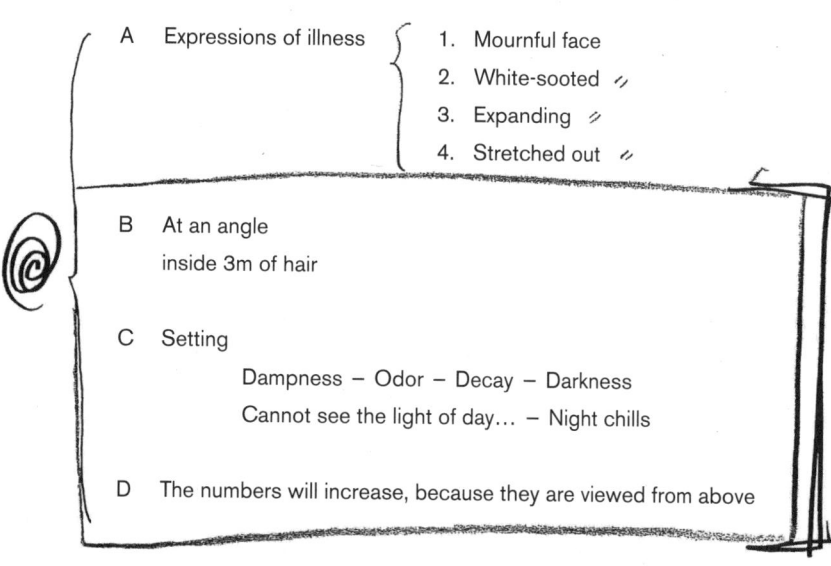

A   Expressions of illness
    1. Mournful face
    2. White-sooted
    3. Expanding
    4. Stretched out

B   At an angle
    inside 3m of hair

C   Setting
    Dampness – Odor – Decay – Darkness
    Cannot see the light of day… – Night chills

D   The numbers will increase, because they are viewed from above

Note: Grapple with the <u>movements of each fragment</u>
    so they don't get lost in the abstract atmosphere

〈舞首〉

鬼がガキみたいに乾いている　キバを忘れるな

1.　口より火を吹く　左下（キバと上目）
2.　小太郎的キバ　　上
3.　　　　　　　　　右足元

⟨ Maikubi ⟩

Demon as dry as a Gaki   Don't forget the fangs

1. Blow fire from mouth   lower left (fangs and upward glance)
2. Kotarō-ish fangs   up
3.   by the right foot

7　　　　　　　　　　　1

（化けヒナ鳥　）

　畳の上、口の中にゲンコを入れられたニワトリが逃げまわる

　地ゴクに

(Ghost Chick)

On the tatami, chicken with a fist shoved into its mouth runs this way and that

To hell

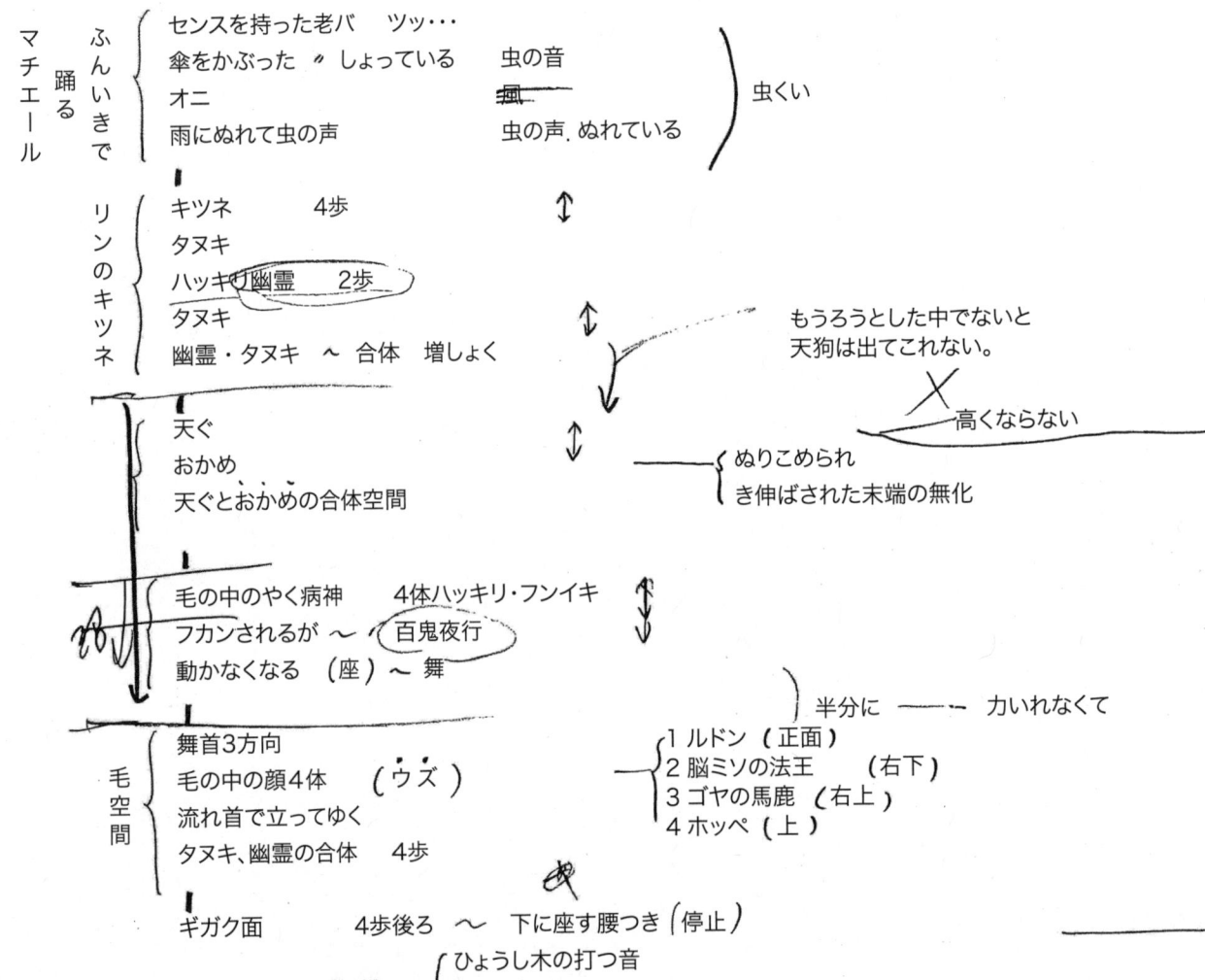

ビア   そうぜつな嵐
　　　　ちょうりつ

〈 順番を超えたゆうがさ 〉
　動きの流れの必然性

　　　　　※　1. 高低がない
　　　　　　　2. 舞首のつながり　　─ ♪ 止まらず、流れ
　　　　　　　3. 天グの理解　　　　─ 前にのびるもの、後ろにのび
　　　　　　　　　　　　　　　　　　るもの、ひきさかれる空間
　　　　　　　4. やく病神の理解
　　　　　　　　　　　　　　　　　─ 表情ハッキリ、関わる
　　　　　　　　　　　　　　　　　　ものに関わった時出てくる
　　　　　　　　　　　　　　　　　　もの
　　　　　　冷気を吹って
　　　　　　　　日の目をあびられない
～～～～～～～～～～～～～～～～～～～～

━面を空間化する
　前に伸る、長い鼻、後頭に伸びてひきのばされるもの
　末端神経の無化

　　　　◎　雨、ヤキ

━{ カラカラに乾いている
　　口がさけている（歯は出てもよい）

~~Solo 1~~ YAMAMOTO   (Setting) { Phosphorus – Decomposition – Backbone of a ghost body
Neon sign – Cough – Decay – Breath – Foxfire

Bring closer to things that hang in the air

@ A well-established setting is important

Matière / Dance with the air of
{ Old woman with folding fan   tsss… [walking on tiptoes]
" with open umbrella on her back   Sound of insects
Demon   ~~Wind~~   ) Insect-eaten [gradually chewed away]
Wet with rain and sound of insects   Sound of insects. Wet }

Phosphorus fox
{ Fox   4 steps
Raccoon dog
Precise ghost   2 steps
Raccoon dog
Ghost – Raccoon dog ~ merge propogate

Tengu unable to emerge
unless in a hazy stupor

Tengu [long-nosed goblin]
Okame [ugly, good-natured woman]
Space of merged Tengu and Okame

{ Rubbed in
Annihilation of […] Stretched out extremities

✗ Do not go high

Yakubyōgami inside mass of hair   4 iterations, precisely – atmosphere
Viewed from above, but… ~ (Hyakki Yagyō)
Cease to move (seated) ~ dance

Half strength ——— not too forceful

Hair Space
{ Maikubi in 3 directions
4 iterations of Face in hair   (vortex)
Come to standing, with drifting necks
Raccoon dog and ghost merge   4 steps

{ 1 Redon (en face)
2 Pope of Brains (lower right)
3 Goya's Idiot (upper right)
4 Cheek (above)

Gigaku masks   4 steps back ~ sit with hips down, downstage (stop)

{ Sound of wooden clappers
Quietness

Bia   — Sublime storm

— Tuning

⟨ Grace transcends sequential order ⟩
⟨ Necessity of the flow of movement ⟩

1. No level change
2. Maikubi connections   —   flow, unstopping
3. Understanding of Tengu   —   that which stretches forward, that which stretches backward, space that is torn apart
4. Understanding of Yakubyōgami   —   clear expression, that which appears when engaged with the matter of concern

Blowing cold air
Cannot feel the light of day

{ Make the surface three-dimensional
The long nose stretches forward, like something is stretched and pulled behind the head
Annihilation of nerve extremities

Rain ,   *Yaki*

{ Parched dry
Mouth is torn (teeth can be seen)

金魚と衣装

{ アリアドーネ　　（空間の糸にからまる）
　ビアズレ婦人　　　粒子と臭い、けだるさ
　正面のクジャク婦人　　　　ひょう変

{ 腰の羽
　銀の針のスネイク　（トイエン使って）
　　〜 回転

{ 植物空間　{ 足元より茎
　　　　　　　〜腰の葉 〜肩の葉 〜耳の重い実
　　　　　　　（暗い表情で下る）

　海坊ズ　{ フカン
　　　　　　毛だらけ

　柳（立ってゆき）
　野花（粒子のパチパチ）

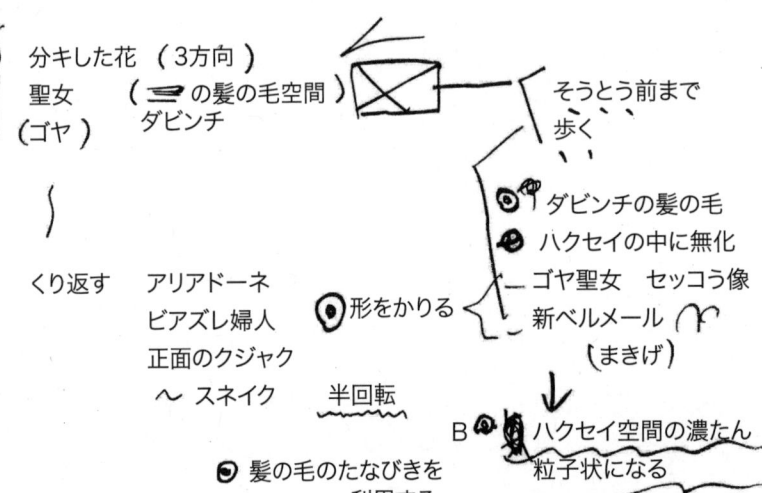

{ 分キした花（3方向）　　　　　　　そうとう前まで
　聖女　（ーの髪の毛空間）　　　　　歩く
　（ゴヤ）　ダビンチ

　　　　　　　　　　　　　　ダビンチの髪の毛
　　　　　　　　　　　　　　ハクセイの中に無化
　くり返す　アリアドーネ　　　ゴヤ聖女　セッコウ像
　　　　　　ビアズレ婦人　　形をかりる　新ベルメール
　　　　　　正面のクジャク　　　　　　　（まきげ）
　　　　　　　〜 スネイク　　半回転
　　　　　　　　　　　　　　　　B　ハクセイ空間の濃たん
　　　　　　　　　　　　　　　　　粒子状になる
　　　髪の毛のたなびきを
　　　利用する

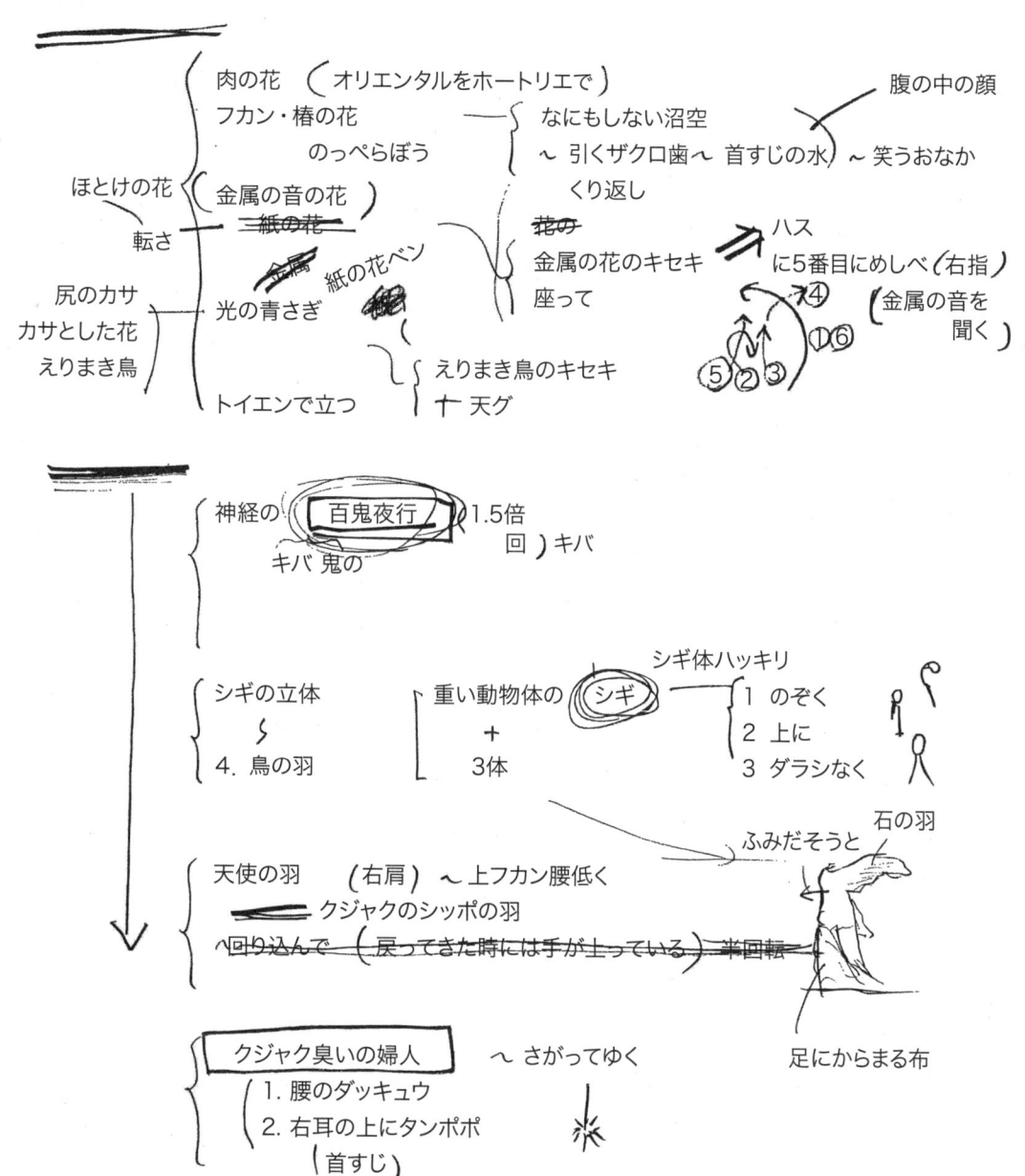

Solo 2 GOLDFISH AND COSTUME

{ Ariadne   (tangled with the threads of space)
  Madame Beardsley (particle and odor, sluggishness
  Madame Peacock in front   Sudden transformation

{ Wings on the waist
  Silver needle snake (use Toyen)
        ～ rotations

{ ● Plant Space   { Stem grows from underfoot
                    { ～ Leaves at the waist ～ Leaves around the shoulders ～ Heavy-eared fruit
                    (descend with a mournful expression)

  Umibōzu [ocean ghost] { View from above
                         { Hair all over

  Willow (stand and go)
  Wildflowers (*pachi pachi* [crackly sound] of particles)

{ Flower that has branched off (in 3 directions)
  Saint   (Space of ⇌ hair)   Walk
  (Goya)   Da Vinci's   quite a ways up to the front

                                                 ● Da Vinci's hair
                                                 ● Annihilation in taxidermy
  Repeat   Ariadne   Saint Goya   Lady in plaster
           Madame Beardsley   ● Borrow the shape   New Bellmer ⌒
           Peacock en face   (curls)
               Snake ～ Half-rotation   ↓
                                                 B ● ● Concentration of Taxidermy Space
           ● Use the trailing wisps of hair   Reduced to particles

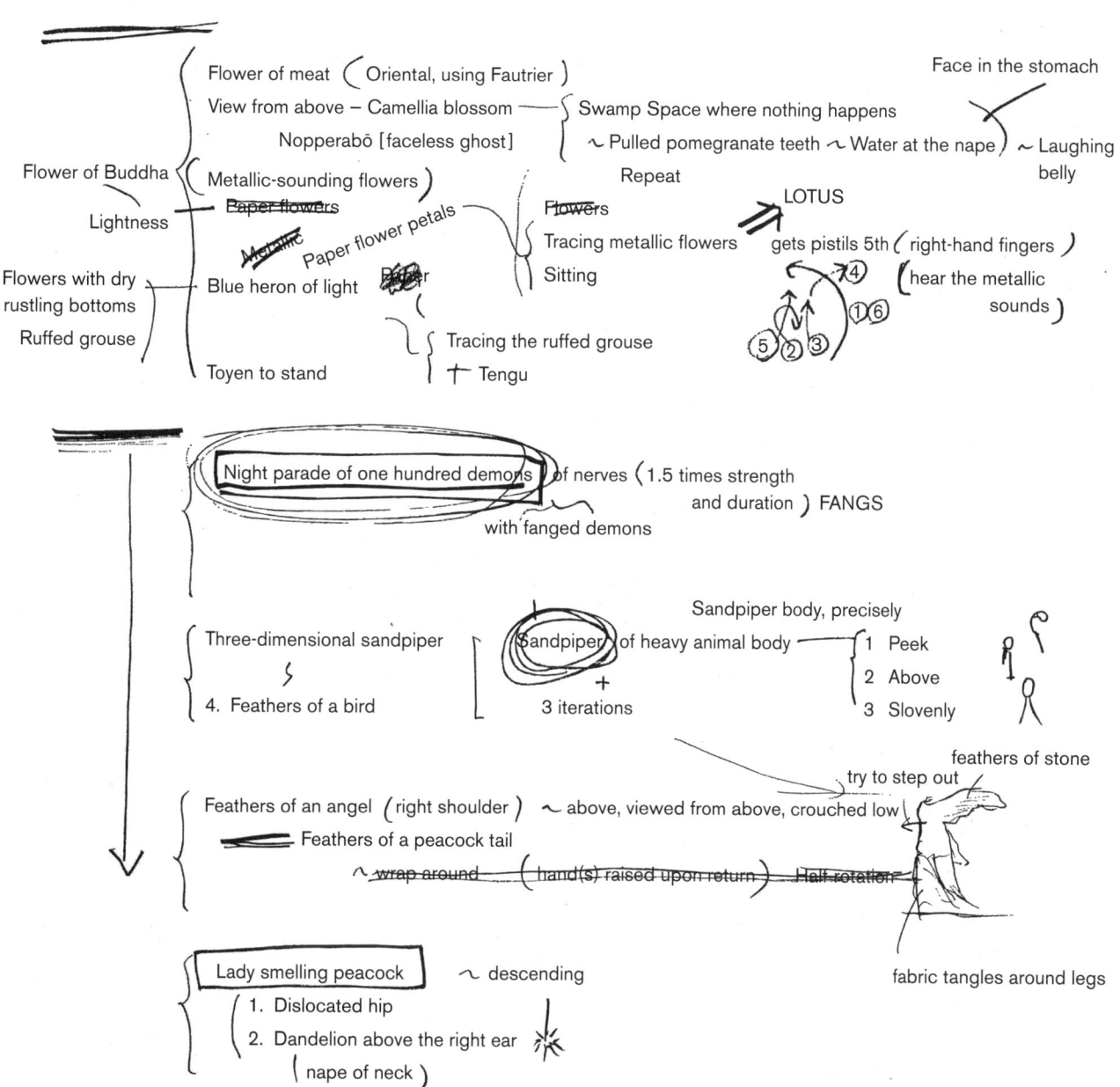

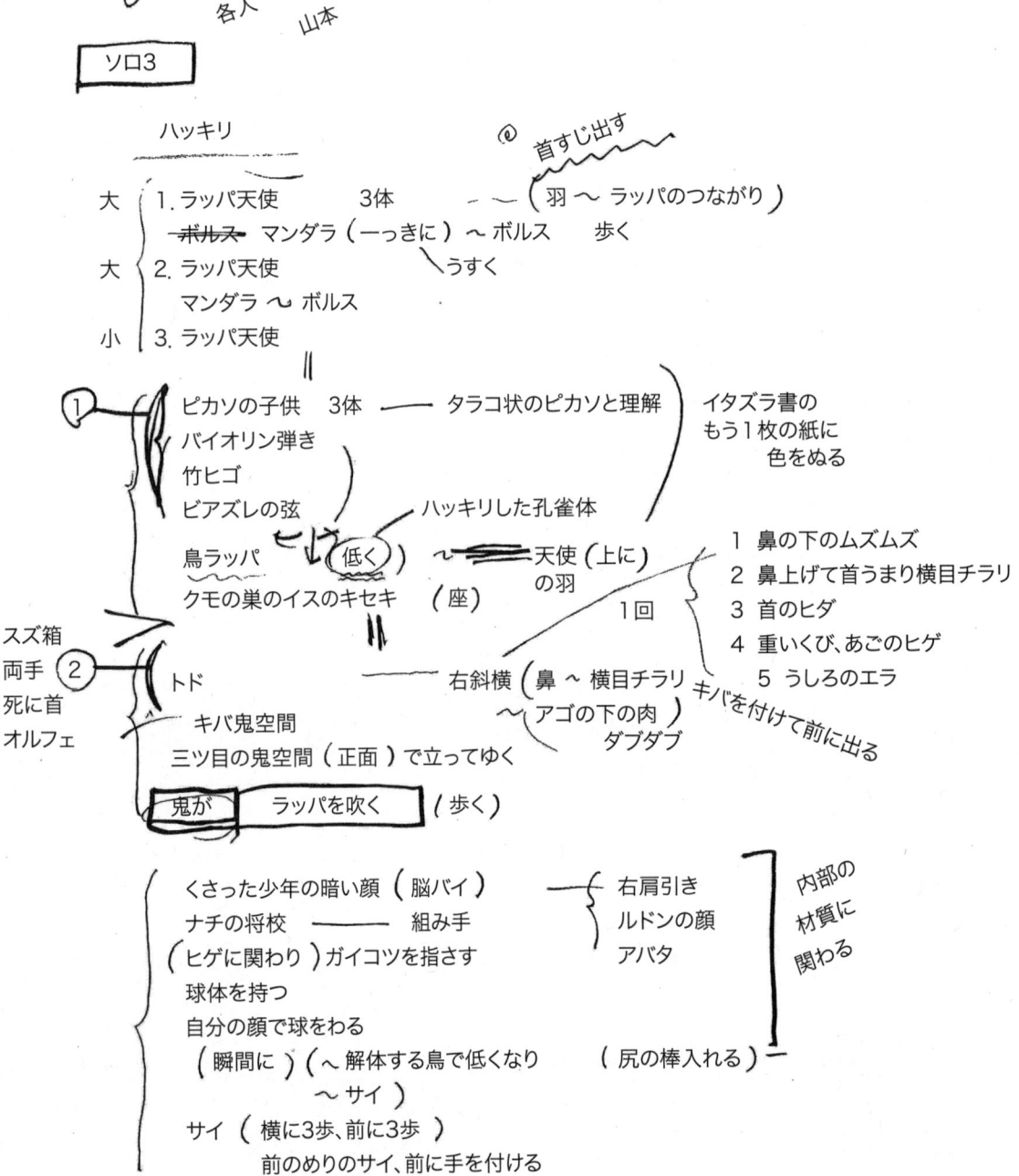

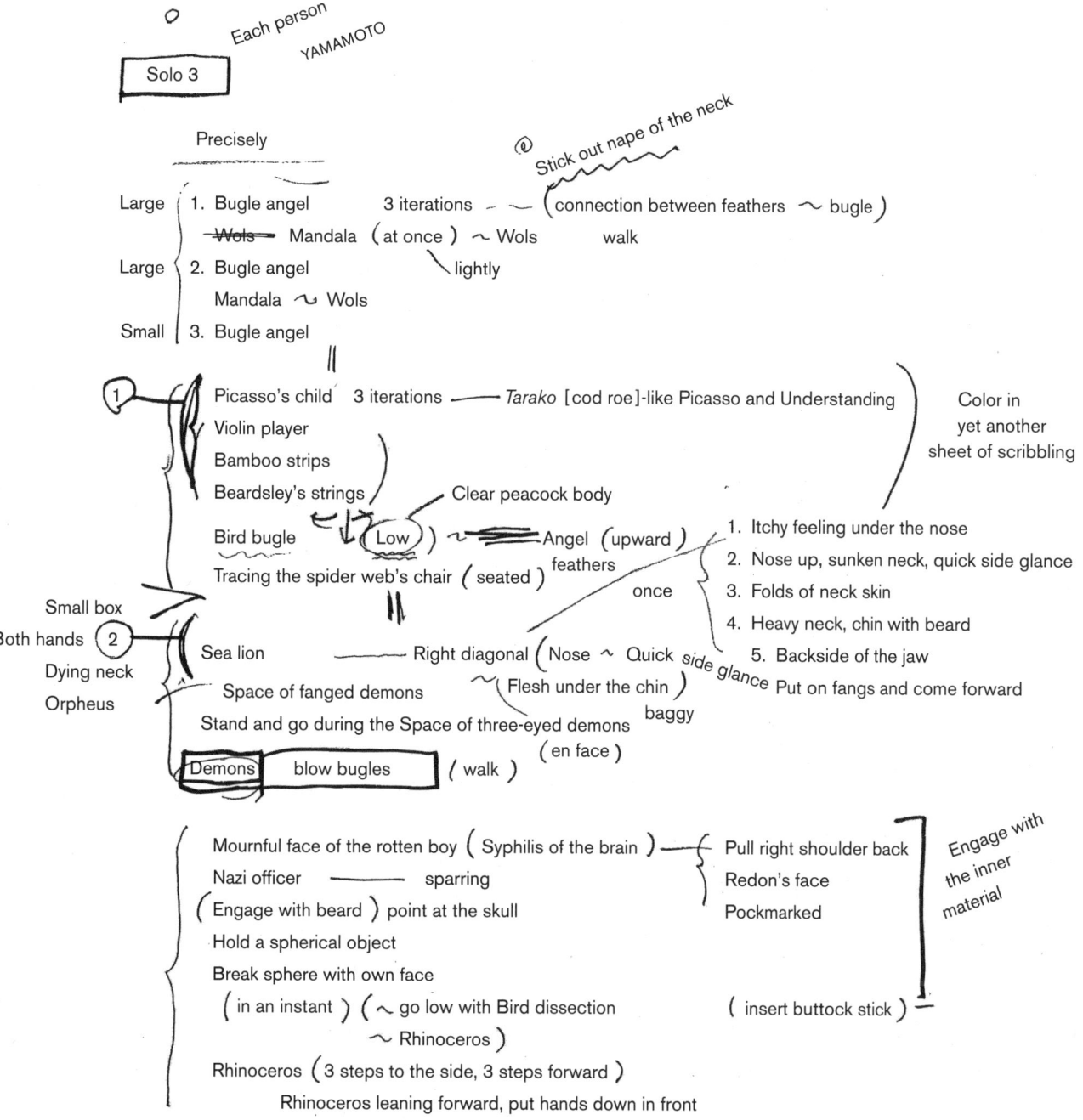

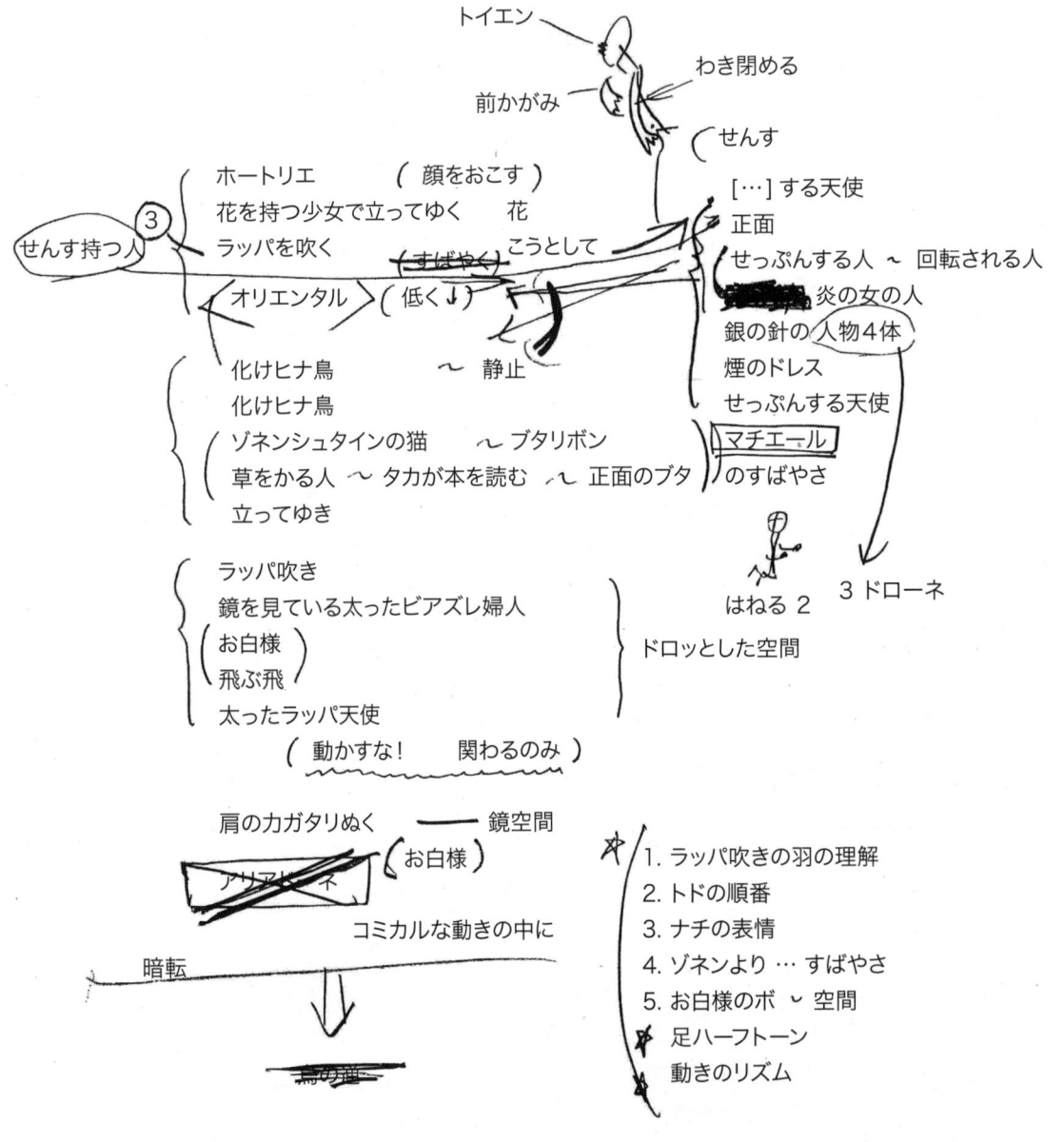

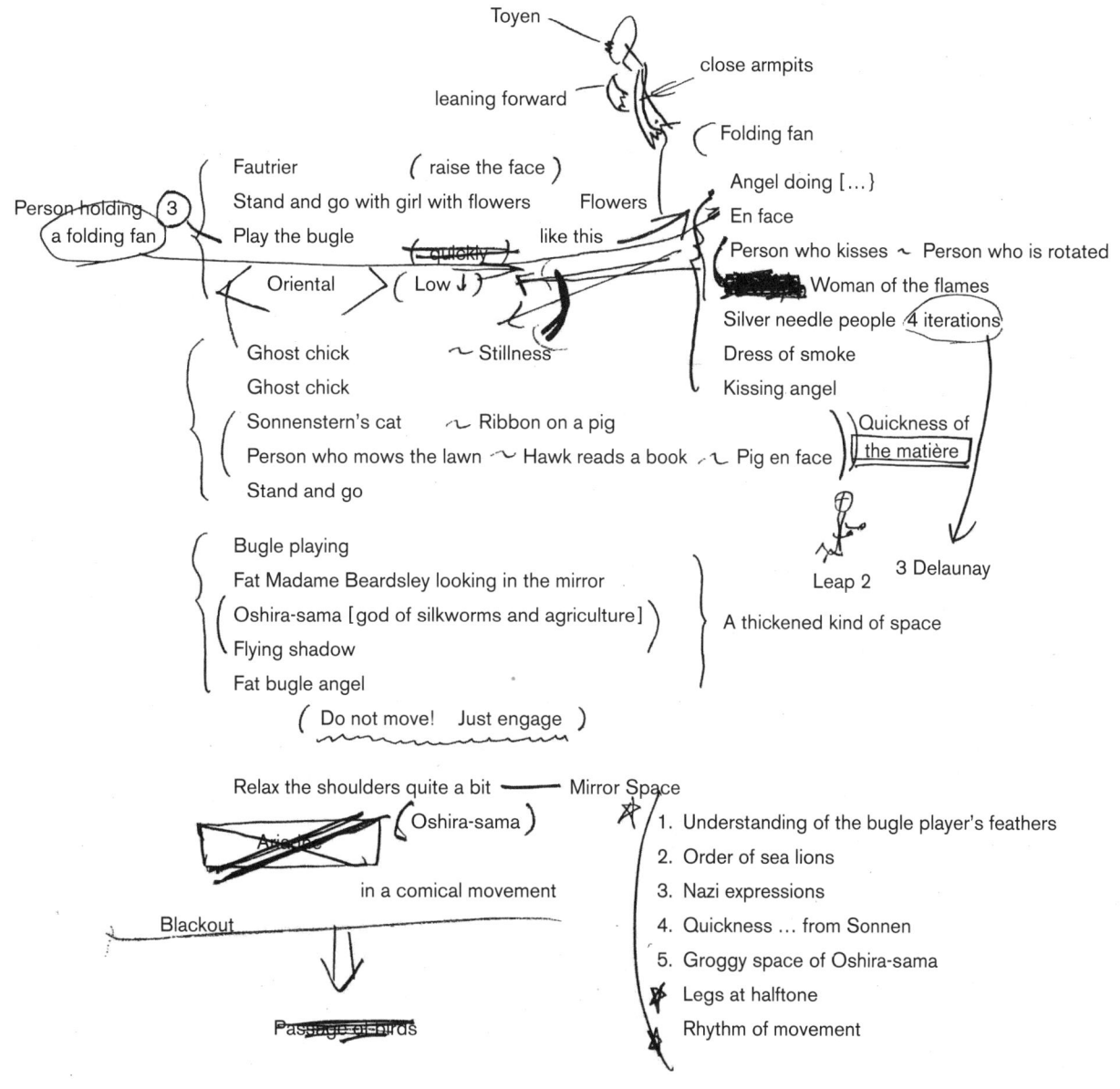

　　　　　Q　　　　　　　　　　　　　　　　　　　　　　子供のダッチョウおしめ ────

　ソロ4　　　横田

　　　　　　　　　　　　　　　　　　　　　　　　　↑
　　　　暗いバラ　　4歩　　　　右手にせんす　　神経のクラクラ
　　　　フカン　　　　　闇のとばりがおりてゆく
　　1　ゴヤの老婆
　　　　しかめ面の老婆
　　2　ゴヤの老婆
　　　　しかめ面
　　　　バウロ
　　3　ゴヤ
　　　　暗いバラ大将 ├ すけたバラ ）

　　　　人魚（日をあびる）髪の毛いじる
　　　　すすけた人（まな板に刃もの）
　　　　ときわ　2体　　　　　　　　　　　指伸ばしてヒラヒラ
　　　　手の扇　　（口の中に呼び込む、左）
　　　　顔に手の扇
　　　　船　　あそび　　1　右手の扇上に
　　　　　　　　　　　　2　左手の2本指そえる
　　　　　　　　　　　　3　左手のせんすのあそび
　　　　口の中にせんす
　　　　左腕のたもとを上げる
　　　　左手であおぐ　　パタパタ（尻にあおぐ）
　　　　クジャク（尻の風がひろがり）
　　　　バラの少女
　　　　フカン　～　長い尾のクジャク

　　　　かゆいキツネ
　　　　キツネをだく老人
　　　　長いツメを持った~~老人~~馬

38

―――― 坊主がよく似合う

{ フカン ～ 大井河（のぞく人）
  くさった少年の顔
  (フカン) ～ 中ブの人が四ツンバイで歩く

  フグリをいじる ~~子供~~ 女
  ふとんにうもれた子供 ～ 指をなめる ――{ 小指より ～ 親指
                                       ～ 顔のキセキを取る

  海の中をおよぐ   { 海そう取り ～ もぐる
     （足のパタパタ）   { 海そう ～ 大きくおよぐ √(羽つかって) もぐる
                         海そう ～ クロール ～ 横およぎ ～ 海そう
                         波が打ちよせる ～ 岩に乗る

胸をたたく子供   ～ パタン

ザクロ歯でゴリラ   １   腰に羽

{ うるし塗り { 大きいハケ   ～   小さいハケ
               おけの中で回る ～ カンザシつけてカタン
  船頭　で立ってゆき   おけしょう
  逃げる老婆　（曲折で逃げる）
       ↑↗
       カター

Solo 4   YOKOTA   Hernia diapers for children ———

⎧ ⸻ Mournful rose ⸻   4 steps   Folding fan in right hand   Dizziness of nerves
⎪   View from above   A shroud of darkness descending
⎪ 1 Goya's old woman
⎪   Scowling old woman
⎨ 2 Goya's old woman
⎪   Scowling
⎪   Paolo
⎪ 3 Goya
⎩   ⸻ Mournful Rose General ⸻ (Transparent rose)

⎧   Mermaid (basking in the sun)   Mess around with hair
⎪   Soot-covered person (knife on the cutting board)
⎪   *Tokiwa* [unchanging stones]   2 iterations   ⎫ Stretching fingers, fluttering
⎪   Fan with the hand (wave into the mouth – left)   ⎬
⎪   Fan with the hand, to the face   ⎭
⎨   Boat   games   ⎛ 1 Right-hand fan, up
⎪   ⎜ 2 Add two fingers from left hand
⎪   ⎝ 3 Fan in left hand, play
⎪   Folding fan in mouth
⎪   Raise the left sleeve
⎪   Fan with left hand   *pata pata* [fan flapping] (wave over buttocks)
⎪   Peacock (buttock wind spreading)
⎪   ⸻ Girl with roses ⸻
⎩   View from above ∼ Peacock with long tail

⎧ Itchy fox
⎨ Old person hugging fox
⎩ Old ~~person~~ horse with long nails

———— The bald head becomes you

View from above　～ Ōigawa [peeping tom]
Face of rotten boy
(View from above)　～ Palsied person walking on all fours

~~Child~~ Woman fondling testicles
Child buried in blankets　～ lick fingers　———(from the pinky finger ～ thumb
　　　　　　　　　　　　　　　　　　　　　　　　 ～ trace the outline of the face

Swimming in the ocean　　　 Collect seaweed ～ dive under
(legs *pata pata* [flapping])　Seaweed　～ swim with large strokes ～ dive under (using feathers)
　　　　　　　　　　　　　　　　Seaweed ～ forward crawl ～ sidestroke ～ seaweed
　　　　　　　　　　　　　　　　Lapping waves　～ get on the rocks

Child beating chest　～ *patan* [sound of something shutting]

Gorilla using Pomegranate teeth　　1　　Feathers on the waist

Lacquering　　　　　　　Large brush ～ small brush
　　　　　　　　　Spinning inside the bucket ～ put on the hair pin and *katan*
Stand and go with　Boat　Head　　　　　　　　　Makeup
Old woman running away (run away meandering)

kataa—

（正面より）

せっぷんする人　〜　される人
　　　　　　（回転する間に変る）

炎の中の女の人　　　（田中傘）
　｛ねじれ
　　分キする体　　ゆがみ
　　銀の針
　〜　ドレス煙の女

せっぷんする天使

　　　　　　　トットッ歩く

　〜　下見る
　〜　左前方

五月の花ムコ　　→　ゴヤのマチエールをすべて
　　　　　　　　　体の中にたくわえる

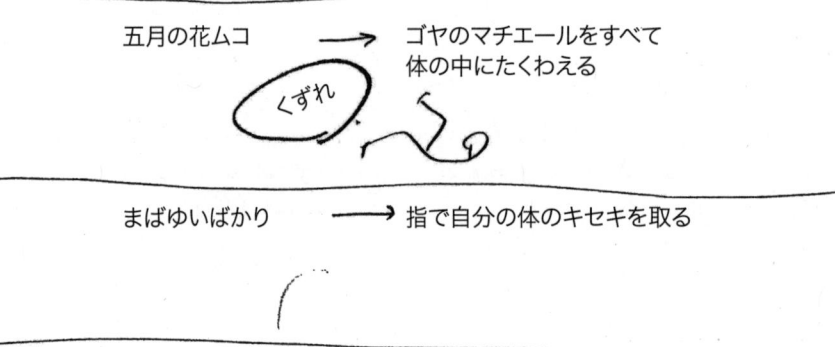

まばゆいばかり　　→　指で自分の体のキセキを取る

ホートリエの材質　人物 3体
　　　〜　森の中の顔　のくり返し　すすけた人物

(from the front)

Person who kisses ⁀ who is kissed
(change while rotating)

Woman in the flames   (Tanaka umbrella)
{ Contortion
  Body branching off   Distortion
  Silver needle
⁀ Dress   Woman of smoke

Kissing angel

                            Walk *totto* [quickly]

⁀ Look down
⁀ Forward left

Groom in May   →   Stash in the body
                           all the matières de Goya
(Crumbling)

Blindingly   →   Trace own body's shape with finger

Fautrier's material People 3 iterations
    ⁀ repetition of   Face in the woods   Soot-covered person

```
⎛ ゴリラ                          歩く馬鹿
⎜ 馬鹿
⎜ ウサギ
⎜ どびんを持つ
⎜ 老婆
⎜ かんめし    （頭大な頭）
⎝〜 らせんのウズ   足カター


⎛ すかし見る  〜（ 内ゾ ）
⎜ 喰べる子供   〜
⎜ 泣く子供    〜
⎜ 眠り       〜
⎜ キセルをすう 〜             タラコ
⎜ ホテイ      〜
⎜ 小判ジャラジャラ 〜
⎜ 眠        〜
⎝ せんす


    クジャク
```

⎧ Gorilla   Walking Idiot
⎪ Idiot
⎪ Rabbit
⎨ Hold the teapot
⎪ Old woman
⎪ Meal in a can (Enormous head)
⎩∼ Spiral vortex   Legs *kataa* [break apart]

⎧ See through   ∼ (Internal organ)
⎪ Eating child   ∼
⎪ Crying child   ∼
⎪ Sleeping   ∼
⎪ Smoking a pipe   ∼
⎨ Hotei [god of abundance and happiness] ∼   *Tarako*
⎪ Gold coins jangling   ∼
⎪ Sleep   ∼
⎪ Folding fan
⎪
⎩ Peacock

孔雀　　乗
　　歩く馬

Peacock   Ride
            Walking horse

フラマンの幽霊

十二相A ｛ 透かし見る　〜　内臓
　　　　　 喰べる子供　〜　〃
　　　　　 泣く子供　　〜　〃
　　　　　 眠り　　　　〜　〃

ヒョウで伸びる

十二相B ｛ キセルを吸う　〜　〃
　　　　　 ほてい　　　〜　〃
　　　　　 小判ジャラジャラ（∥恵寿様）〜　〃
　　　　　 眠り　　　　〜　〃
　　　　　 せんす　　　〜　〃

ヒョウ　〜　透し見る

歩く馬鹿 ｛ 手ブラブラのゴリラ　　〜　横向き　〜　しわくちゃ老婆の顔
　　　　　 馬鹿
　　　　　 ウサギ
　　　　　 どびんを持っている
　　　　　 老婆がの後へのぞきこむ
　　　　　（巨大頭部）
　　　　｛ ラせんが体の中に入る
　　　　　 左足カタン　〜　上に伸びる　　　真横に出ている

Flamman's Ghost

Group of 12 movements
A
$$\begin{cases} \text{See through} & \sim \text{Internal organ} \\ \text{Eating child} & \sim \quad '' \\ \text{Crying child} & \sim \quad '' \\ \text{Sleep} & \sim \quad '' \end{cases}$$

Stretch using Panther

Group of 12 movements
B
$$\begin{cases} \text{Smoking a pipe} & \sim \quad '' \\ \text{Hotei} & \sim \quad '' \\ \text{Gold coins jangling} \;(\text{\textbar\textbar}\, \text{Ebisu-sama [god of fishermen and merchants]}) & \sim \quad '' \\ \text{Sleep} & \sim \quad '' \\ \text{Folding fan} & \sim \quad '' \end{cases}$$

Panther $\sim$ See through it

Walking Idiot
$$\begin{cases} \text{Gorilla with arms hanging free} \quad \sim \quad \text{Facing sideways} \sim \text{Wrinkled face of old woman} \\ \text{Idiot} \\ \text{Rabbit} \\ \text{Holding a teapot} \\ \text{Old woman peeks behind her} \\ (\text{Massive head}) \\ \begin{cases} \text{Spiral goes into the body} \\ \text{Left leg } \textit{katan} \sim \text{ stretch upward} \quad \text{Protrude straight to the side} \end{cases} \end{cases}$$

ソロ　　　　武将　　（かぐや）

- やけどの天使 — 4歩 — かさぶたとして登場
  停止5つ

- 体の中よりクモの巣　　　花
  ドレスを持ち上げる　　　薄いまく

- 光の中の女曲芸師 —
  1. 右手の星のパラパラ
  2. 両手のカギ
  3. つなひき
  4. ミニオン
  5. 眠り

  ビニールの薄い槽状の果樹園
  　　　　ゆっくり

- 光のハクセイで　ゴヤの人物　4体 —
  1. 盲の背ズイカリエス
  2. 合掌する子供
  3. 光のしゅうげきによる —— 光の化物
  4. ベーコンの付着より剥離（体細く）

  ～ 剥離のままさがり
  ほえる　　（～その中に眠りとなって後ろ向き） — 背すじのばす
  セッコウの婦人像

- 〈回り込んで正面〉
  子供の顔のフクロウ —
  おいらん一体
  メンコ（口のカクカク）で前に出る
  1. フクロウ
  2. 変な鳥 — シッポ
  　　　　　　トサカ
  - 恐怖でぬり込め
    横目チラリ
    髪の毛つかってメンコ

- 振動より臭いの連続
  小春1体
  1. 鼻に耳
  2. 自分の臭い
  3. 左右のガス

Solo

Commander (Kaguya)

{
- Angel of burns — { 4 steps / Pause for 5 } — { Enter as a scab
- Spider web from within the body   Flowers
- Lift up dress   Delicate layer
}

{
- Female acrobat in the light — {
  1. Right-hand stars *parapara* [scattering]
  2. Keys to both hands
  3. Tug of war
  4. Mignon
  5. Sleep
  }
- Orchard in the form of a thin plastic layer
  slowly
}

{
- Goya's characters in a taxidermy of light 4 iterations — {
  1. Spinal decay of the blind
  2. Child with hands in prayer
  3. Monster of light —— resulting from an attack of light
  4. Detaching from attachment to Bacon (with a thin body)
  }
- ～ descend while peeling off
- Bark (～ turn back at that moment as an instance of sleep) —— straighten the spine
- Image of a lady in plaster
}

{
- ⟨Circle around and come to the front⟩ { 1. Owl
- Owl with a child's face ———————— 2. Strange bird — { Tail
- Courtesan, one iteration ——————————————— Cockscomb { fill in out of fear
- Come to the front with *menko* [card-slapping game]   quick sideways glance
  (*Kaku kaku* in the mouth)   *menko* using hair
}

{
- Succession not of vibrations, but smell — {
  1. Ears to nose
  2. Your own smell
  3. Gas to either side
  }
- *Koharu* [geisha song], 1 iteration
}

{聖歌隊　　　　　————————　上の神経
　髪の毛百鬼のちょっとした低迷より
　神経、イタミの孔雀で首たっけい

蛇をのみこんだ獣（トド）

$\left\{\begin{array}{l}\text{Choir} \quad\text{————————}\quad \text{Nerves from above}\\ \text{From the slight stagnation of one hundred demons of hair}\\ \text{Nerves, neck crucifixion with peacock of pain}\end{array}\right.$

Beast that swallowed a snake (sea lion)

〈 コブ 〉
　　　　コブで歩く（登場）

　　　　　1. 刀を持つ人　（八幡太郎）
　　　　 ｛ 2. 玉を　〃　　　　　　　　｛ すすけた顔
　　　　　3. いのり　　　　　　　　　　　両手合せる
　　　　　4. 前へつんのめる子供　———　トットッ歩く
　　　　　5. 刀を持つ人B

　✻ デビュフェのアワの人
　★ 形よりマチエール程度

〈 おまけ老婆 〉
　　　　花とベルメール　（ボーとした花 80%）

　　　｛ 笑い（左下）　　〜　沼を通って（内蔵）
　　　　死に首、水に映る（すすけた顔）右下 〜　　〃
　　　　なんでもない顔（正面）　　　　 〜　〃

　　　｛ 羽で上に伸る（神経）
　　　　と苦痛の表情2体　———｛ オメールの猿　（口開け、上目）
　　　　　　　　　　　　　　　　やんでいる子供（口閉じ、目がさかむけている）
　　　〜 フカン

　　　｛ 天使A　　　（左イカクの型）
　　　　　　　　　　笑いより
　　　　くり返し

　　　｛ 天使B
　　　　天使C

⟨ Lump ⟩

    Walk with Lump (Enter)

$\begin{cases} \text{1. Person wielding sword (Hachiman Taro [Japanese commander])} \\ \text{2. \quad\quad\quad\quad ball} \\ \text{3. Prayer} \\ \text{4. Child pitches forward} \\ \text{5. Person wielding sword B} \end{cases}$ $\begin{cases} \text{soot-covered face} \\ \text{put both hands together} \end{cases}$

    ———— walk *totto* [quickly]

✣ Dubuffet's bubbly people
✣ Degree of matière over shape

⟨ Extra old lady ⟩

    Flowers and Bellmer (Spaced-out flowers 80%)

$\begin{cases} \text{Laughter (lower left)} \sim \text{Going through the swamp (Internal organs)} \\ \text{Dying neck reflected in water (soot-covered face) lower right} \sim \\ \text{Ordinary face (en face)} \end{cases}$

$\begin{cases} \text{Stretch up with Feathers (Nerves)} \\ \text{and 2 iterations of expression of pain} \end{cases}$ $\begin{cases} \text{Bellmer's monkey (mouth open, eyes upward)} \\ \text{Ill child (mouth closed, eye hanging off)} \end{cases}$

  ∼ View from above

$\begin{cases} \text{Angel A} \quad\text{(Shape of left intimidation)} \\ \quad\text{(} \quad\quad\text{From laughter} \\ \text{Repeat} \end{cases}$

$\begin{cases} \text{Angel B} \\ \quad\text{)} \\ \text{Angel C} \end{cases}$

もや
指の先の神経　♪で踊る

凝縮された中より立ち上る

Haze
Nerves of fingertips   ) …dance with

Come to standing from a compressed body

　　　　ソロ　　　　　雨宮

⎰ 空を見ている
⎨ 風の流れ4体
⎱ コブのフレーズ

⎰ おまけ老婆
⎨
⎱ トリスタン

⎰ 蛇をのみこんだけだもの　　2体　（トド）
⎨ 〜蛇をすいこみ
⎱ フカンされた花

⎰ クチュクチュの花
⎨
⎨ 両手の植木
⎨ （石の材質で）　鹿
⎨　　　　　　　　チョウチョ
⎱ （マチエル程度の）ブタ

⎰ タマゴ　　　　（振れ〜人さし指〜ラッパ）
⎨ 床にゲリ　　　（手で広げる）
⎱ マンダラ

⎰ 羽のフレーズ　　左羽〜せっぷん（右上）〜右羽〜〃
⎨　　　　　　　　カタカタ（2段階
⎨
⎱

⎰ ずがいを押える（あ〜）
⎨ コブのフレーズ　　⎰ 途中立ちながら
⎨　　　　　　　　　⎱ 後ろ向き
⎱ 流れる後ろ髪の人

Solo   AMAMIYA

{ Looking at the sky
   Flow of wind   4 iterations
   Lump phrase

{ Extra old lady

   Tristan

{ Beast that swallowed a snake   2 iterations   (sea lion)
   ⌢ Sucking in a snake
   Flower viewed from above

{ Crumpled up flower

   Plants in both hands
   (With stone materials)   Deer
                           Butterfly
   (Degree of matière)   Pig

{ Egg   (shake ~ index finger ⌢ bugle)
   Diarrhea on the floor   (spread with hands)
   Mandala

{ Feather phrase   Left feather ∧ Kiss (upper right) ~ Right feather ~ //
                        kata kata [mechanically] (2 levels

{ Press on the skull (Aaaaa ~)
   Lump phrase   { stand midway
                               facing backwards

   Person with hair flowing back

15

新人

{ 単調な手のヒラヒラ　　{ 小人
　　　　　　　　　　　　 脳ミソ
　　　　　　　　　　　　 ゴヤの馬鹿
　　　　　　　　　　　　{ ゲンコをのみこんだ

　けい礼
　（おいでおいでしながら）　手が叉の所に行く
　（くさい嗅いで）

{ 単調な手のヒラヒラ　　〜 同じ
　Ⓑ

　　　　　　　　　　　　{ 口に手
　サル　　　　　　　　　　 左手にエサ
　犬　　（関戸の犬）　　　 横に振動
　　　　　　　　　　　　　 たて 〃

　聖少年
　ダラしない人
　　　　　　　　　　　　{ 指さす人
　　　　　　　　　　　　　 指の振動

{ 煙フクロウ
　一ツ目
　　　　　　　　　　　　　　　　ゲン
　巨人の流れ星　　　　（ビアズレの 絵）
　床に字を書く

NEWCOMER

{ Monotonous hand fluttering { Midget
                                Brain
                                Goya's Idiot
                                Swallow a fist

  Salute   Hand goes to the groin
  (while beckoning)
  (with a foul smell)

{ Monotonous hand fluttering ⌢ same
      Ⓑ

{ Monkey   { hand to mouth
                          food in the left hand
  Dog (SEKIDO's dog) ⎯{ shaking sideways
                          "   vertically

  Young holy man
  Slovenly person
                        { person pointing
                          shaking of the fingers

{ Smoke owl
  One eye   strings
  Shooting stars of giants (Beardsley's 花)
  Write letters on the floor

巨人のパーティー　写真

- ハサミで切っている人
- シギの立体
- グラスを持っている怪獣

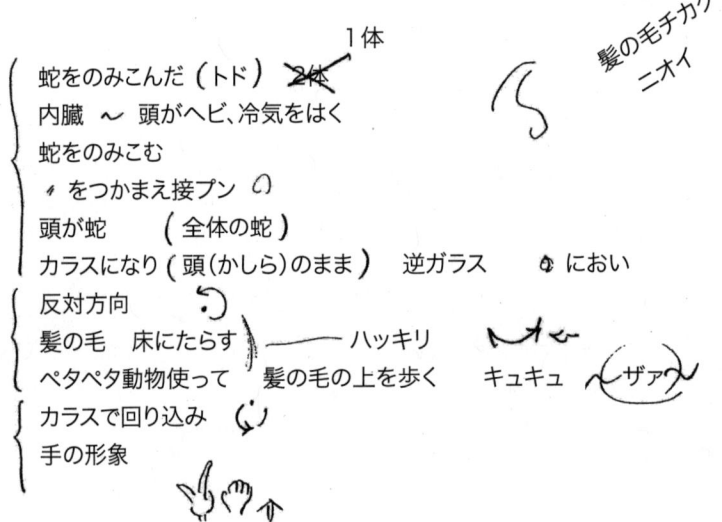

- 蛇をのみこんだ（トド）　~~2体~~ 1体
- 内臓 〜 頭がヘビ、冷気をはく
- 蛇をのみこむ
- ♪をつかまえ接プン
- 頭が蛇　（全体の蛇）
- カラスになり（頭(かしら)のまま）　逆ガラス　におい

- 反対方向
- 髪の毛　床にたらす ——— ハッキリ
- ペタペタ動物使って　髪の毛の上を歩く　キュキュ　ザァ

- カラスで回り込み
- 手の形象

髪の毛チカク
ニオイ

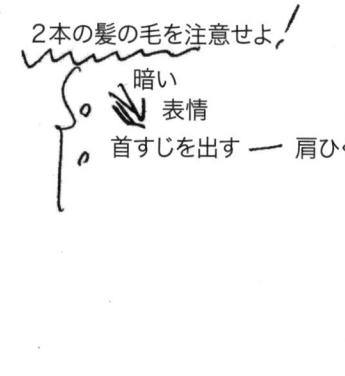

2本の髪の毛を注意せよ！
暗い
表情
首すじを出す ― 肩ひく

Party of Giants   Photograph

{
- Person cutting with scissors
- Three-dimensional sandpiper
- Monster holding a glass
}

{
(Sea lion) swallowed a snake   2 iterations   1 iteration   Hair, near Smell
Internal organs ～ Head is a snake, exhale cold air
Swallow a snake
Capture   and kiss
Head is a snake (whole snake)
Become a crow (head as is)   Reverse crow   smell
}

{
Opposite direction
Hair   hang to the floor) —— precise
Using animals, pattering steps above the hair   Kyu–kyu–   Zaaa
}

{
Come around with crow
Shape of hands
}

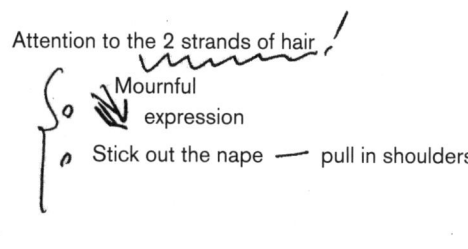

Attention to the 2 strands of hair

Mournful expression

Stick out the nape — pull in shoulders

4

<　病院で日なたぼっこ　>

A　血をはいた病人
・あどけなさ
・鼻血のカサカサ（かさかさ）
・くさった耳
・手の型重要（触覚）

ちょっと左

目玉、見開いている
拡散
今、血をはいたばかり
シャツのよれよれ

B　壁にもたれる病人

斜めにもたれる
おなかくずれ
左手に注意（目をかくす）

C　　せっぷんされている（花子のせっぷん）

　　　　　　　　　　　　　花子の顔のゆがみ
　　　　　　　　　左下
　　　　　口のゆがみ

　　　　頭痛やみの老婆

　　　　　　　　　　　　闇の中に
　　　　　　　　　　　　左の耳

　　　　　　　　　　　　深く痛む

⟨ Basking in the sun at the hospital ⟩

A   Sick person who vomited blood
- Guilelessness
- *kasa kasa* [dryness] after a bloody nose (*kasa kasa*)
- Rotten ear
- Handprint is important (tactility)

slightly left
- Eyeballs, open
- Diffusion
- Just now having vomited blood
- Worn down shabby shirt

B   Patient leaning on wall

- Lean diagonally
- Belly crumbling
- Attention to the left hand (cover eyes)

C   Being kissed (Hanako's kiss)

Distortion of Hanako's face

lower left

distortion of mouth

Old woman suffering from headache

In the darkness

Left ear

Feels deep pain

8 弁当を喰べている少年　　　　肩ごしに下を見ている
　 Young boy eating lunch　　　 Look down over the shoulder

9 まぶしい少女　　　背後の黒　　　　　　強烈な光
　 Blindingly bright girl　Black on the backside　Intense light

9 小山君（下宿の中の男）
　 Mr. Koyama (man in the boarding house)

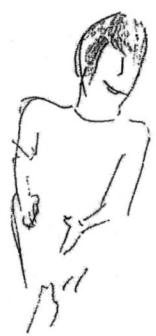

手
Hand

○ 帰る老姿
Old lady returning

○ とくい満面
Proud expression

● ふり返る少女
Young girl looking back

- 雨ガッパの少年　　　　　Young boy in raincoat

- セーラー服の少女　　　　Young girl in sailor-style uniform

- なんでもない少年（性少年）　Ordinary boy (sexual [holy] young man)

心理

- 孔雀の板付き　　4体 ｛ 右
　　　　　　　　　　　　 正面

- 子供　　　　　　4体 ｛ つかまえる
　　　　　　　　　　　　 つかまえられている
　　　　　　　　　　　　 フーセン
　　　　　　　　　　　　 座っている

｛ 円筒形の枯木で立ち上る
　 馬鹿の顔でピカソの解体
　 セリフ「おまえわかっているんだぞ」

　 回り込みザンゲする人
　 ヤジロベ

｛ 箱の手　　　　　　　　　　　　｛ ゼン巻、リズム
　 白面　　　　　　　　　　　　　 千手観音、ぶどうの手 ｝

｛ 沼の百鬼夜行
　 光の人　　（オルフェー）　　　　｛ 左
　 孔雀4体　（左）　　　　　　　　　 正面
　　　　　　　　　　　　　　　　　　 化面孔雀　2歩
　 ~~ハクセイのガブ~~

｛ 強烈なゴリラハス　　　　　　　　｛ 薄く
　 　　　　　　　　　　　　　　　　 ホートリエ
　 (ユニゾン) 兵士の回転　　　　　　 人形の材質に関わって立つ

　 ハクセイのガブ
　 将棋をさす人

PSYCHOLOGY

{ Peacocks already in place when curtains rise   4 iterations   { right
                                                                  en face

{ Child   4 iterations   { Capture
                                    Being captured
                                    Balloon
                                    Seated

{ Stand up with dead cylindrical tree
  Dissecting Picasso with face of Idiot
  Line: "You know it"

  Come around and confess
  Yajirobē [balancing toy]

{ Hand of the box   (Spring – Rhythm
  Sober   Thousand-armed Kannon – Grape hands)

{ Hyakki Yagyō in the swamp
  Person of light (Orpheus)   { left
  Peacocks 4 iterations (left)   en face
                                         Masked peacock 2 steps
  ~~Taxidermy of *gabu*~~
                                         { lightly
  (Intense Gorilla Lotus   Fautrier
                                         Engage with the material of dolls and stand
    Rotation of soldiers (unison))

  Taxidermy of *gabu* [Noh mask]
  Person who plays *shōgi* [Japanese chess]

フクロウ（ブロンズのタカ）　　　　　　１体ハッキリ入れる
片手の羽　　　　　　　　　　　孔雀の１じゅん
高い鳥で立ち上がる　２歩さがる　　枯木

下りたら　カラス　　２体　　（左肩、右肩）
（４段階の落下）
高い鳥　　〜（４段階の落下）

下りたら　　　　スプーンの老婆
（〜リズムに乗って上下 〜 右回り ↻ ）

高い鳥
後へさがって戸板に付着

Owl   (bronze hawk)   1 iteration   insert precisely
Single-hand feathers   Hesitation of peacocks
Stand up with Birds up high   2 steps back   Dead tree

After descending   Crow   2 iterations   (left shoulder, right shoulder)
    (4 levels of descent)
Birds up high   ∼ (4 levels of descent)

After descending   Old woman with spoon
(∼ up and down on the rhythm   ∼ turn to the right ↷)

Birds up high
Go back and attach to the back gate

「金魚」　 にじの衣装

さらし首　　　　　　　　　　　　　　銀の針の理解

｛ センスを持った老婆　　　　　　　　　 高さを変えない
　 ギガク面　　　　　　　　　　　　　　ますます低くなって広がる

｛ とけて　　回り込み後ろ髪の幽霊
　 シッポをささえる子供（尻出す）
　 後ろ髪の幽霊　　　　　　　　　　孔雀
　　　　　　　　　　　　　　　　　 首カッカッ使って

｛ アリアドーネ
　　　　　　　　　　　　　　　　　　 光る心姿なし
　　　　　　　　　　　　　　　　　　 スネイク回るじゅんびなし
　 孔雀婦人　　　　　　　　少しさがる

｛ 武将

　 ほえる　後ろ向きのセッコウ婦人

｛ 白鳥
　 ピアノ弾き
　 ボッカチオの婦人　　→　衣装をぬいでゆく

⌐GOLDFISH¬   ☞Rainbow costume

Pilloried neck   ◉ Understanding of silver needles

{ Old lady with folding fan   ⎧ ● No level change
  ʃ   ⎨
  Gigaku masks   ⎩ ○ Go even lower and spread out

{ Melting   Ghost with hair flowing in back comes around
  Child supporting tail   (buttocks out)
  Ghost with hair flowing in back ——⌠ Peacock
                                    ⌡ Using the neck *ka ka* [angular]

{ Ariadne
  ʃ   ⎧ ● Shining heart, no figure
                                        ⎨ ● Snake turn with no preparation
  Madame Peacock   ------- go down a little

{ Commander
  ʃ
  Barking ⌒ Lady of plaster looking backward

{ Swan
  Piano player
  Madame Boccaccio   ⟶ removing costume

```
 ⎧ 後ろにねがえり              線          視線の解体    3方向の重層
 ｜ 体のこしたまま半分ねがえり  空間        かみの毛空間            くもの巣
 ｜ ちじまるねむり             表情        子供十二相
 ⎩ ねがえろうとして正面                    （女なだれあめ）← ねがえりうつ子供
           （芸者）                         髪の毛にからまれる女 〔炎の中の女〕
                    ● 寝わざの踊り          足カタン       芸者
                        ⎧                  もうろうとした女（ほどける女）
  水中                   ｜   暗い少年
 ・ひじでささえない       ⎨     柳の無化      視線解体
 ・のびきらない          ｜
 ・芸者はハッキリ、正面すかす   柳空間   →   衣裳を腰にかけ立とうとする
──────────────────────────────────────────────
          ⎧  口のカクカク
          ｜  脳ミソ 〜 ヨダレ
          ⎨  さく乱の小動物      （蛇・トド）   暗い幽霊
          ｜                                    かみの毛
          ⎩

          ⎧  武将    子供の顔フクロウ
          ｜        恐怖でぬり込められて横目チラリ
          ｜        髪の毛つかってメンコの女形
          ⎨        メンコ口カクカク
          ｜        振動より臭いの連続
          ｜        小春1体
          ｜        聖歌隊
          ｜        髪の毛百鬼の低迷より
          ⎩        痛みの孔雀たっけい
```

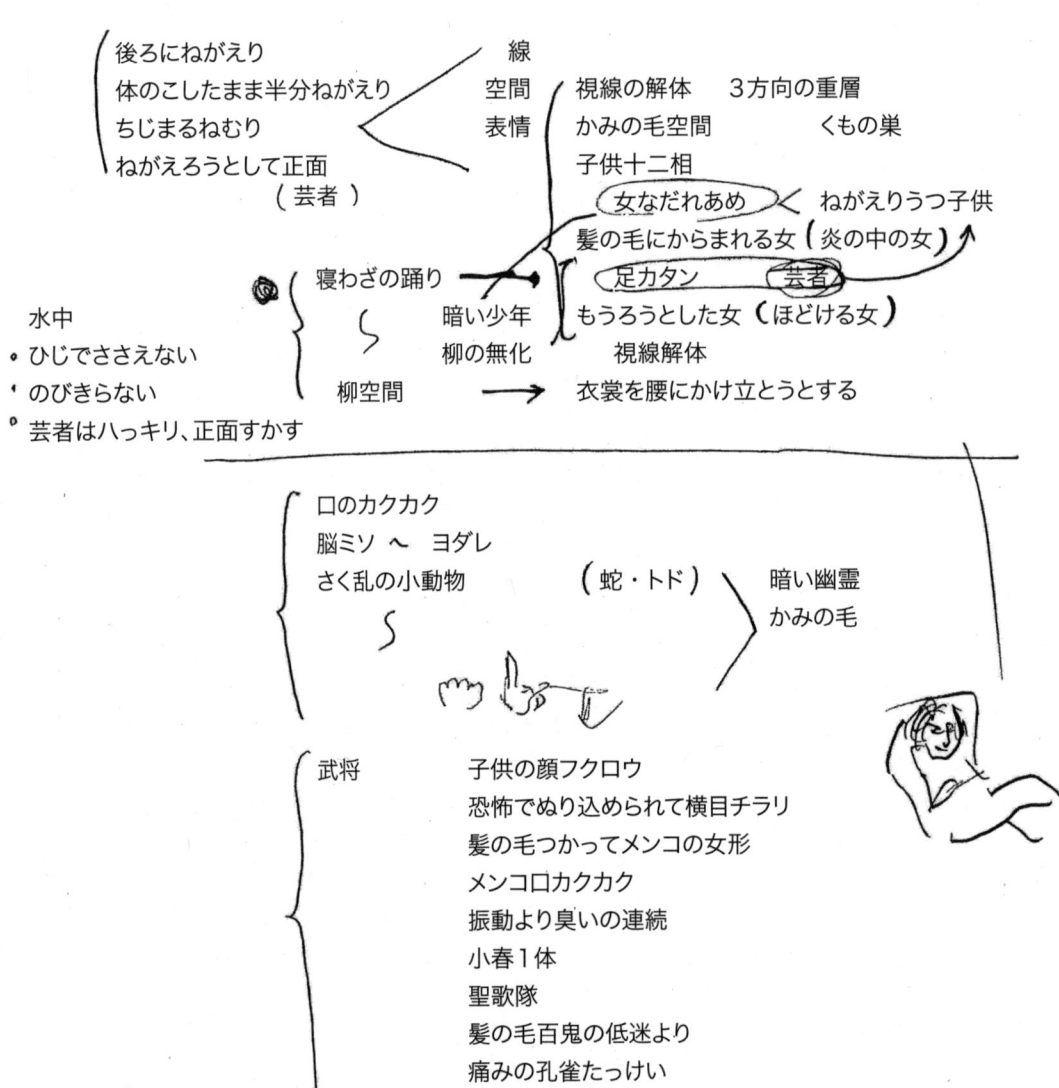

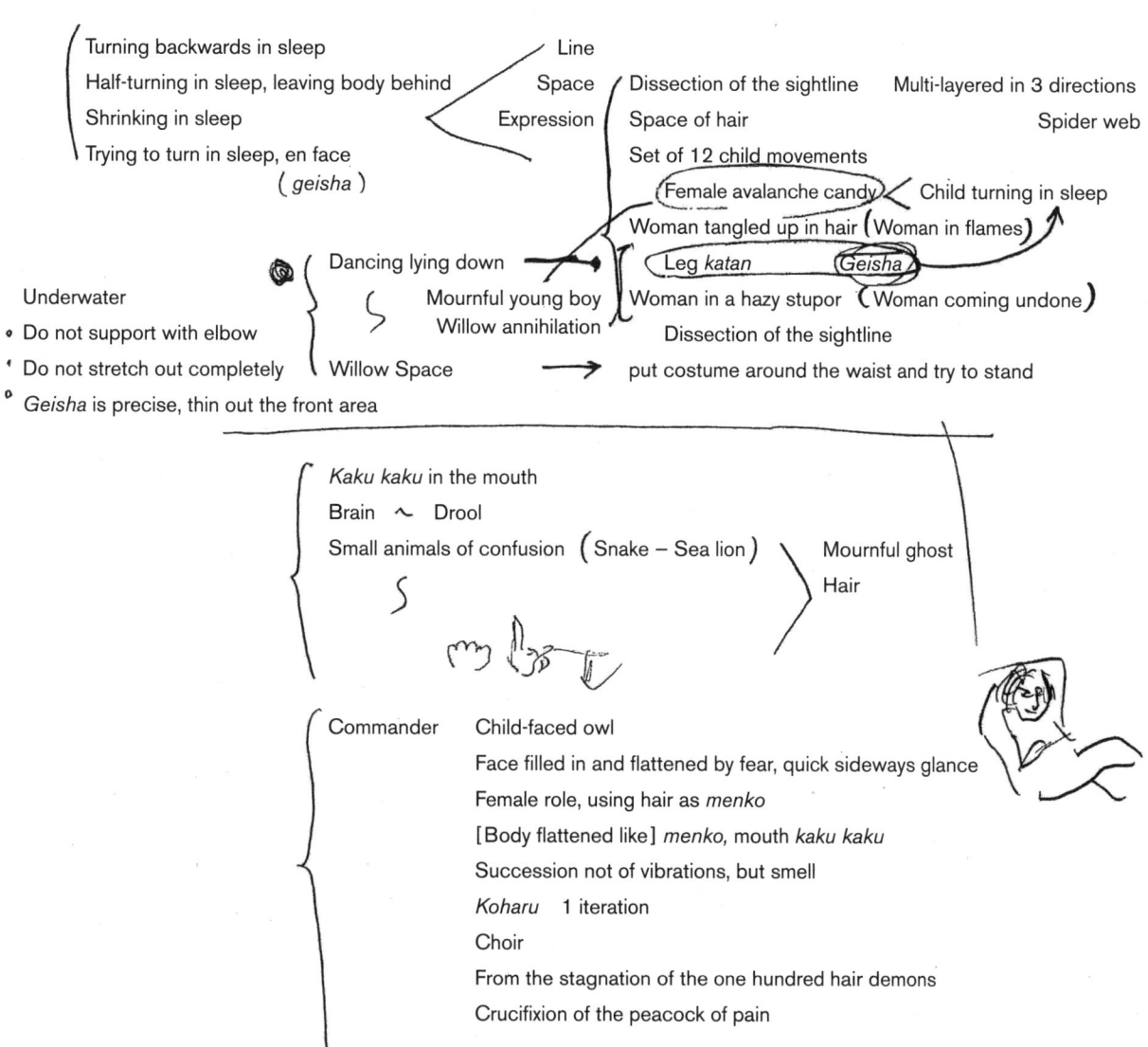

「 チューリップ 」　　　白衣裳　　（ドレス）

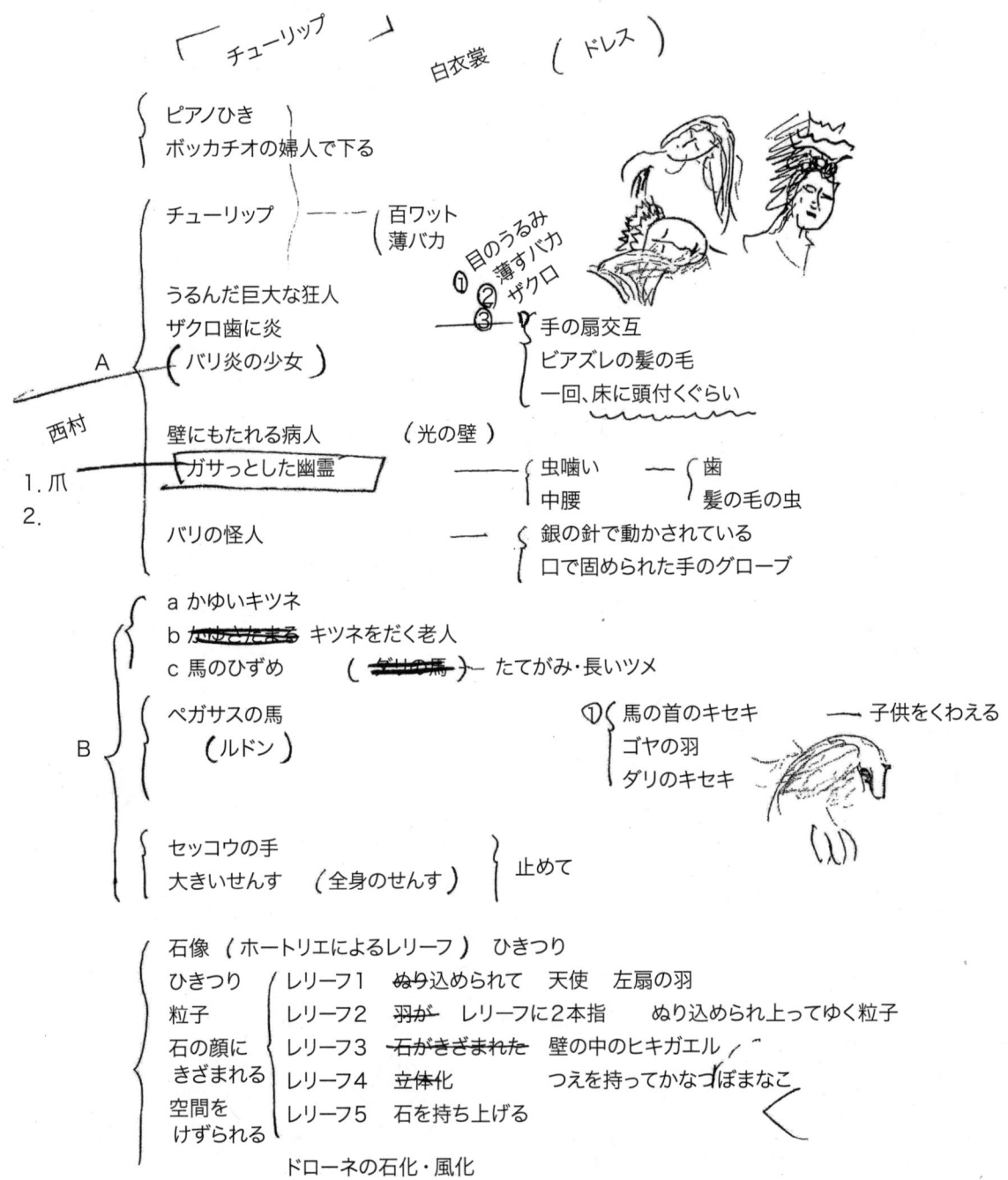

```
           ┌ ピアノひき
           │ ボッカチオの婦人で下る
           │
           │ チューリップ ─ ─ ─ 百ワット
           │                    薄バカ       ①目のうるみ
           │                                 ②薄すバカ
           │ うるんだ巨大な狂人                ③ザクロ
       A   │ ザクロ歯に炎                    ─ 手の扇交互
           │ （バリ炎の少女）                   ビアズレの髪の毛
           │                                 一回、床に頭付くぐらい
   西村    │
           │ 壁にもたれる病人　　（光の壁）
 1.爪      │ ガサっとした幽霊  ──┬ 虫噛い ── ┬ 歯
 2.        │                      └ 中腰      └ 髪の毛の虫
           │
           │ バリの怪人         ── ┬ 銀の針で動かされている
                                   └ 口で固められた手のグローブ

           ┌ a かゆいキツネ
           │ b かさたまる キツネをだく老人
           │ c 馬のひずめ （ダリの馬） たてがみ・長いツメ
           │
       B   │ ペガサスの馬             ①┬ 馬の首のキセキ ── 子供をくわえる
           │ （ルドン）                 │ ゴヤの羽
           │                           └ ダリのキセキ
           │
           │ セッコウの手
           │ 大きいせんす （全身のせんす） ┤ 止めて

           ┌ 石像 （ホートリエによるレリーフ） ひきつり
           │ ひきつり     レリーフ1  ぬり込められて 天使 左扇の羽
           │ 粒子         レリーフ2  羽が レリーフに2本指 ぬり込められ上ってゆく粒子
           │ 石の顔に     レリーフ3  石がきざまれた 壁の中のヒキガエル
           │ きざまれる   レリーフ4  立体化 つえを持ってかなつぼまなこ
           │ 空間を       レリーフ5  石を持ち上げる
           │ けずられる
           │              ドローネの石化・風化
```

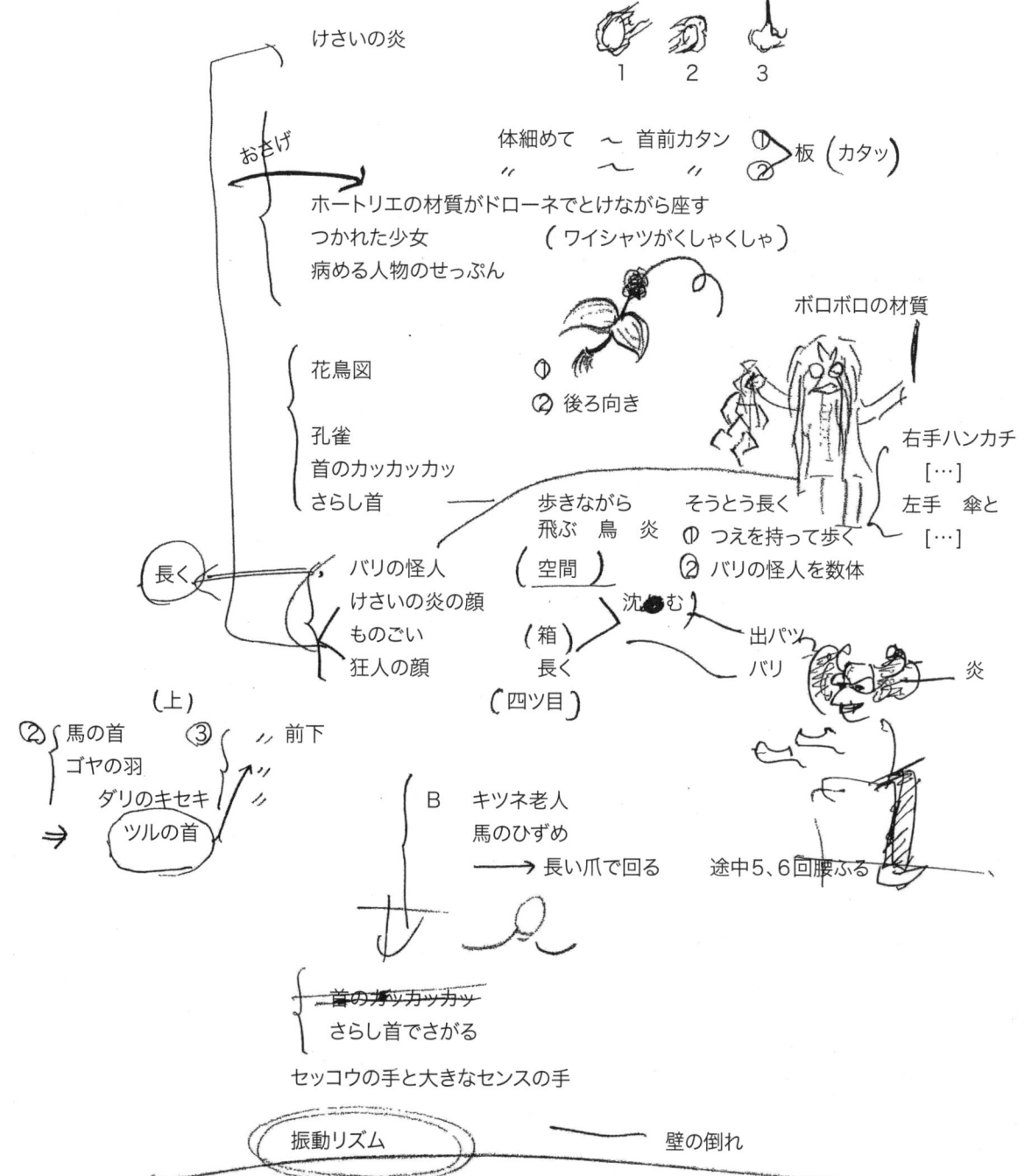

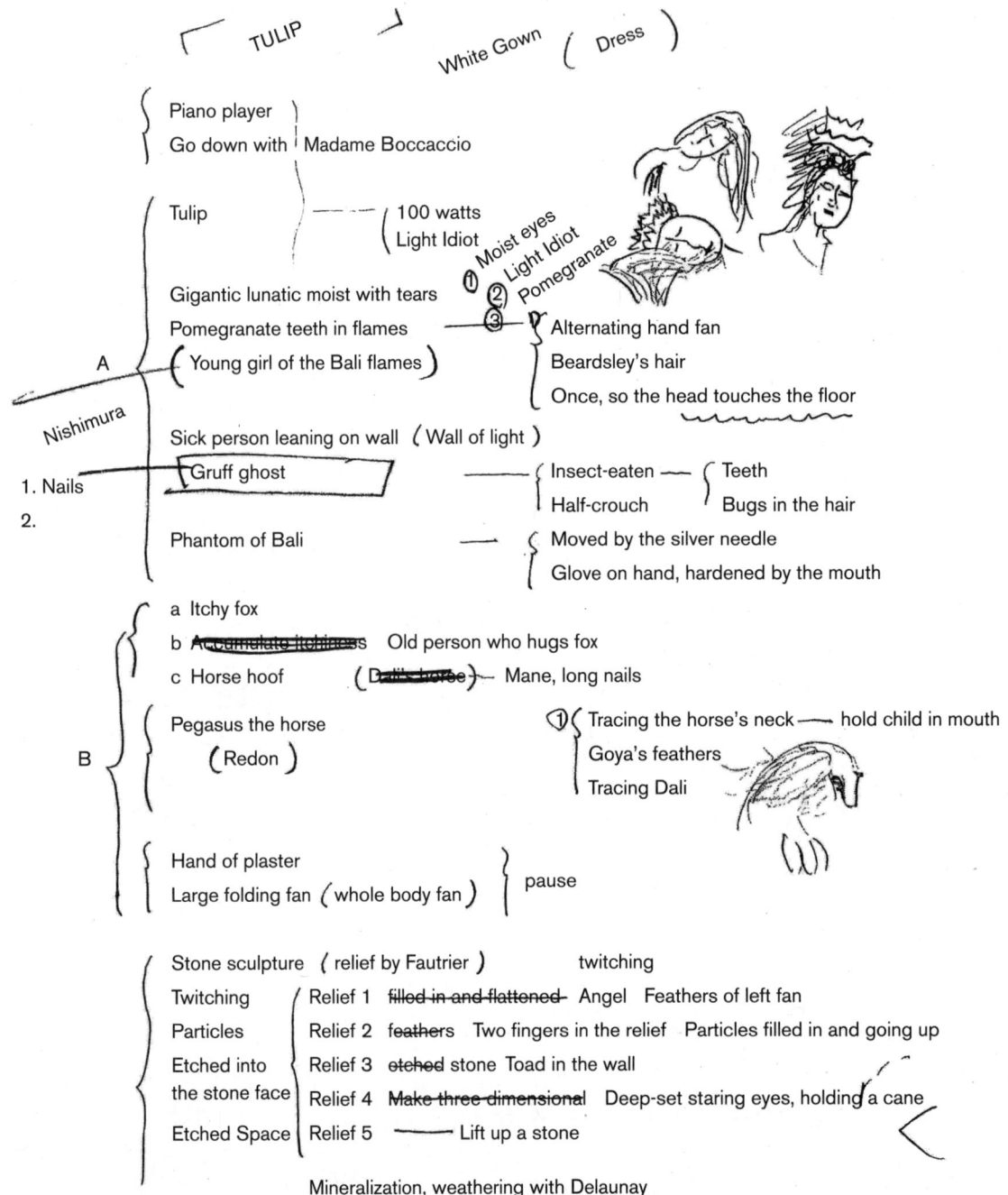

┌ TULIP ┐   White Gown (Dress)

```
          ⎧ Piano player  ⎫
          ⎨ Go down with │ Madame Boccaccio
          ⎩               ⎭

            Tulip          ───── ⎧ 100 watts
                                 ⎨          Moist eyes
                                 ⎩ Light Idiot  Light Idiot
                                      ① 
                                      ②            Pomegranate
            Gigantic lunatic moist with tears    ③
            Pomegranate teeth in flames  ─────  ⎧ Alternating hand fan
   A                                            ⎨ Beardsley's hair
          ( Young girl of the Bali flames )     ⎩ Once, so the head touches the floor

Nishimura   Sick person leaning on wall ( Wall of light )

1. Nails    ┌Gruff ghost              ─────  ⎧ Insect-eaten ──── ⎧ Teeth
2.          └─────────────┘                  ⎩ Half-crouch       ⎩ Bugs in the hair

            Phantom of Bali           ─────  ⎧ Moved by the silver needle
                                             ⎩ Glove on hand, hardened by the mouth

          ⎧ a  Itchy fox
          ⎪ b  ~~Accumulate itchiness~~  Old person who hugs fox
          ⎩ c  Horse hoof       ( ~~Dali's horse~~ ) ── Mane, long nails

   B        Pegasus the horse              ①⎧ Tracing the horse's neck ──── hold child in mouth
          ( Redon )                         ⎨ Goya's feathers
                                            ⎩ Tracing Dali

          ⎧ Hand of plaster            ⎫
          ⎨ Large folding fan ( whole body fan ) ⎬  pause
          ⎩                            ⎭

          ⎧ Stone sculpture ( relief by Fautrier )        twitching
          ⎪ Twitching    ⎧ Relief 1  ~~filled in and flattened~~  Angel  Feathers of left fan
          ⎪ Particles    ⎪ Relief 2  ~~feathers~~  Two fingers in the relief  Particles filled in and going up
          ⎨ Etched into  ⎨ Relief 3  ~~etched~~ stone  Toad in the wall
          ⎪ the stone face⎪ Relief 4  ~~Make three-dimensional~~  Deep-set staring eyes, holding a cane
          ⎪ Etched Space ⎩ Relief 5  ────── Lift up a stone
          ⎩
                      Mineralization, weathering with Delaunay
```

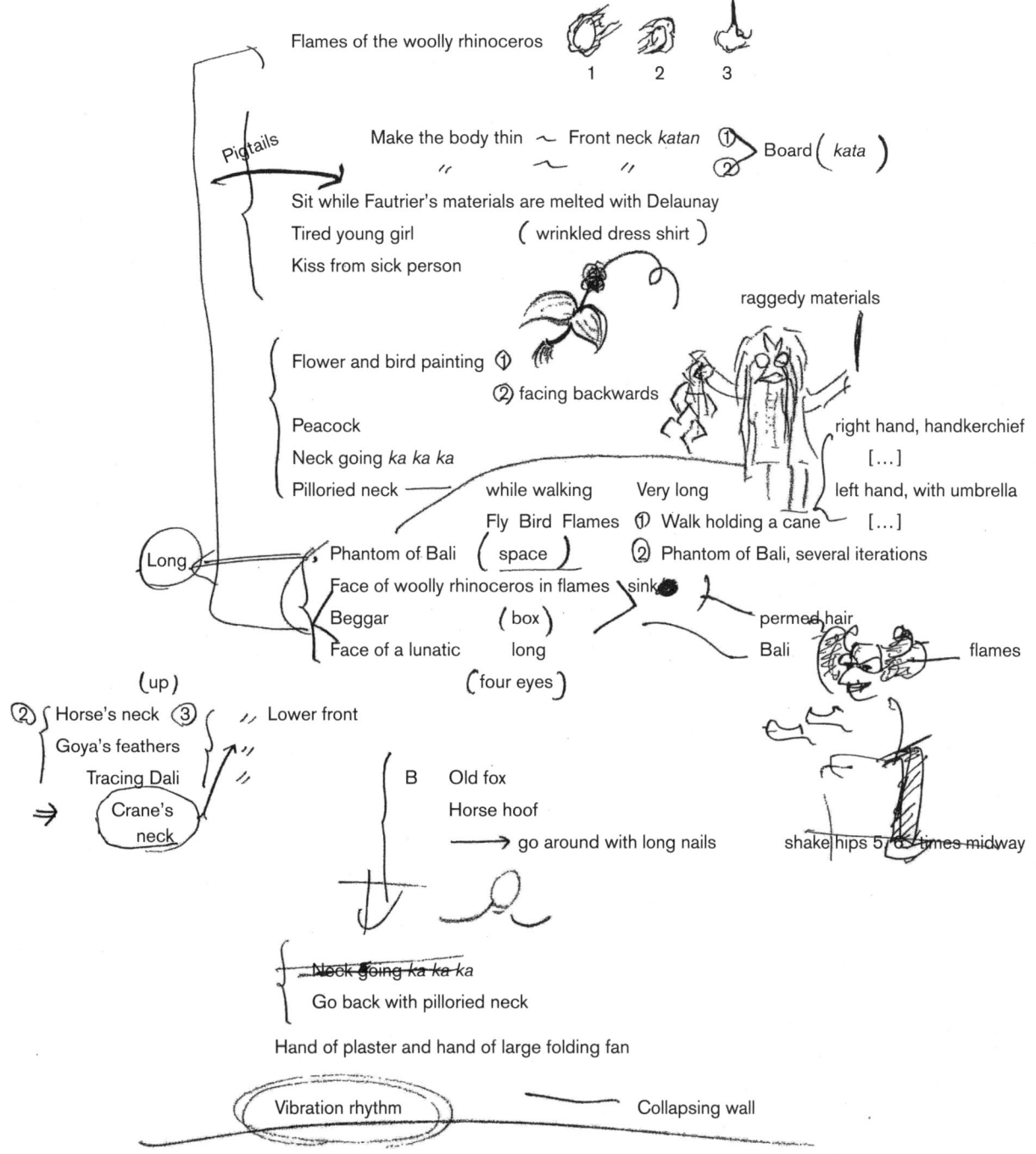

(17夜)
10/18

14

幕明　[レースの場面]

　　㊥　音 ── 口の中にかすかな歌
　　　　アラー ── [せっこう体] で出てくる　　　〜さがる
　　　　　　　　　　　　　　　〜2回目
　　　　アラー
　　　　　　　せっこう体出て　　〜そのまま座る　　　[座った
　　　　　　　バリの神様　~~ヤリを持つ神へ~~ →　 全員 ~~神様~~
　　　　　　　全員飛んでいるヤリ　　　　　　　　　　一人うす馬鹿]
　　　　　　　　　　　　(立って同じ型)
　　　　　　　　せっこうの顔に戻り　出たり入ったり ── 消える

　　●→ 浅田　ソロ

────────────────────────────

[クシの場面]
　　　　　　　　　　　　　　　　ソロモン王宮　〈半分〉
　①　鯨線のベーコン・ユニゾン
　　　　　　　　　　　↓
　　　　　　　　　　(横田ソロ)　　　イカクゴリラ(部1)、マヌカン(部2)
夜　　[孔雀心理]　　　　　　　　　　ゾンネ、ベーコンで引っぱる
　　　　　　　　　　ユニゾン1/3 ──● 横田 { およぎ始めて ─(孔雀)
　②　ベーコン(ソロモン王宮)　　　　　　　頭いじって　　右向の孔雀
　　　　　　　　↓　　　　　入る
　　　　　　　(小田ソロ) ── 花ぞの
　　　　　　　　　　　＜　　通過
　　　　　　　　　　　　●── 最後孔雀のひきつりで後さがり　　　●通過
　　　　　　　　　　　　　　(高い鳥)

────────────────────────────

　{ ⓐ 浅田　　　　ⓑ ベーコンの中に柔らかい動き入れる
　　ⓑ 新人3人　　　(くしの場面)
　　ⓒ ロウソク？

(17 Nights)   14

10/18

Beginning [Lace Scene]

{
Sound ──── Slight song in the mouth
Allah ──── Come out with [body of plaster] ～ go back
                                         ～ 2nd time

Allah
Body of plaster comes out ～ sit as is
God of Bali (to the God of Spears) → | All gods are seated |
Everyone a flying spear | One slight Idiot |
    (stand in the same shape)
Return to plaster face   come and go ── (disappear)
}

→ ASADA solo

─────────────────────────

[Comb Scene]
                              ── Court of Solomon (half)

① Bacon on the Whale String, unison
        ↓
      (YOKOTA solo) → Gorilla intimidation (part 1), Mannequin (part 2)
                       Pull with Sonnen, Bacon
Night [Peacock psychology] unison 1/3 ──→ YOKOTA { Beginning to swim ── Peacock
② Bacon (Court of Solomon)   { Messing with the head ── Peacock facing right
        ↓   Enter
      (Koyama solo) < Flower garden
                      Pass   • Pass
           ──────────────• End, go back with the twitching peacock
                            (Bird up high)

─────────────────────────

{ ⓐ ASADA   ⓐ Insert soft movement in Bacon
  ⓑ 3 newcomers   (Comb Scene)
  ⓒ Candles ?
}

　　　　⎡サイの場⎤── 精神病院
　　　　⎣　音　⎦── ブキ
　　　　　　　　── 馬のさけび ─ ひずめ

⎧　一頭の馬　　（小山）
⎪　馬小屋　　（かたまり出てくる）── ~~馬さがる~~ 僧侶
⎪　　　　　　　　　　　馬のさがり
⎨　　　　　　　　　　　付着、そのまま場所移動
⎪　　　　　　　　　　　~~サリ~~ ─ a. 空どうの馬
⎪　　　　　　　　　　　フレリチ　b. 鳥
⎪　　　　　　　　　　　　　　　　c. 石の鳥
⎪　　　　　　　　　　　まばゆいばかり ──（中央に集まろうとする）
⎪　　　　　　　　　　　さらし首で散る
⎩

　　和栗のソロ 🍃

　　　山本　　　金魚のソロ　（紅の衣裳）

　──~~途中に藤入る~~────── ~~山本フラマン~~──

　　各人 ── 心理 ────── 最初の孔雀で

⎡Rhinoceros Scene⎤ ── Mental institution
        S(ou)nd ── Weapon
              ── Horse shout ── Hoof

⎧ A single horse (Koyama)
⎪ Horse stable (comes out in a lump) ── ~~Horse goes back~~   Monk
⎪   Horse goes back
⎪   Attach, change location as is
⎪   ~~Relief~~ ── a. Horse in cavity
⎨   Clench   b. Bird
⎪   c. Bird of stone
⎪   Blindingly ── (Try to gather in center)
⎪   Pilloried neck, scatter
⎪
⎪ WAGURI solo 🍃
⎩

   YAMAMOTO   Goldfish Solo (Red costume)

   ~~FUJI enters midway~~   ~~YAMAMOTO Flamman~~

   Each person ── Psychology ━━ With the first peacock

部分　　〔　登場　〕　　　　　

① セッコウ体　　　　各人

　　　　　　　　　陶器の顔　　　　　石コウの材質
　　　　　　　　　　　　　　　　　　囲りの冷えた空気
　　　　　　　　　肩下し　　　　　（ありったけの空間）
　　　　　　　　　右手に傘

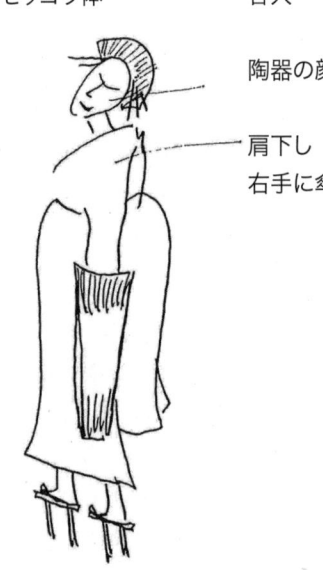

　　　　　　　　　　　　　　　　　　　　　　足のハーフトーン
② ゴヤの聖女　——　肩にかかる三あみ　　　　肩のショールのニオイ
③ 石像　長いおさげ　——　遠くを見ている　　頭のターバン
　　　　　　　　　囲りのクモの巣、柳　〜 回る（後ろ向きで終わる）
④ 大理石の顔　2体　——（光と闇のダビンチ）

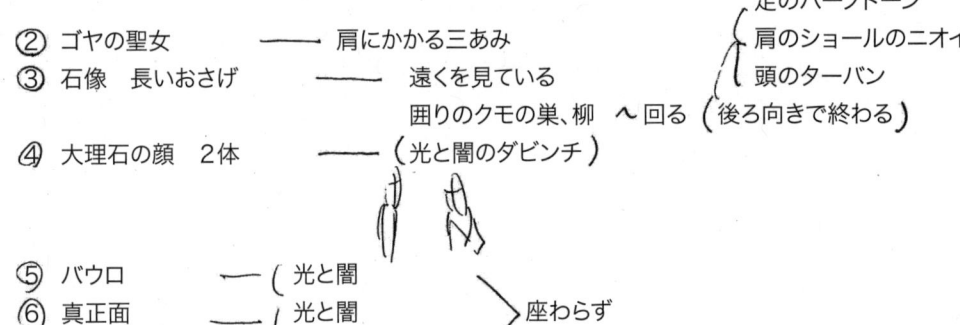

⑤ バウロ　　——（光と闇
⑥ 真正面　　——（光と闇　　　座わらず
　　　　　　　　　（白いライオン

Part   ⟨ Enter ⟩   (3

⓪   Body of plaster   Each person
①

              Ceramic face   Plaster material
                              Cold surrounding air
              Shoulder down   (all the space there is)
              Umbrella in right hand

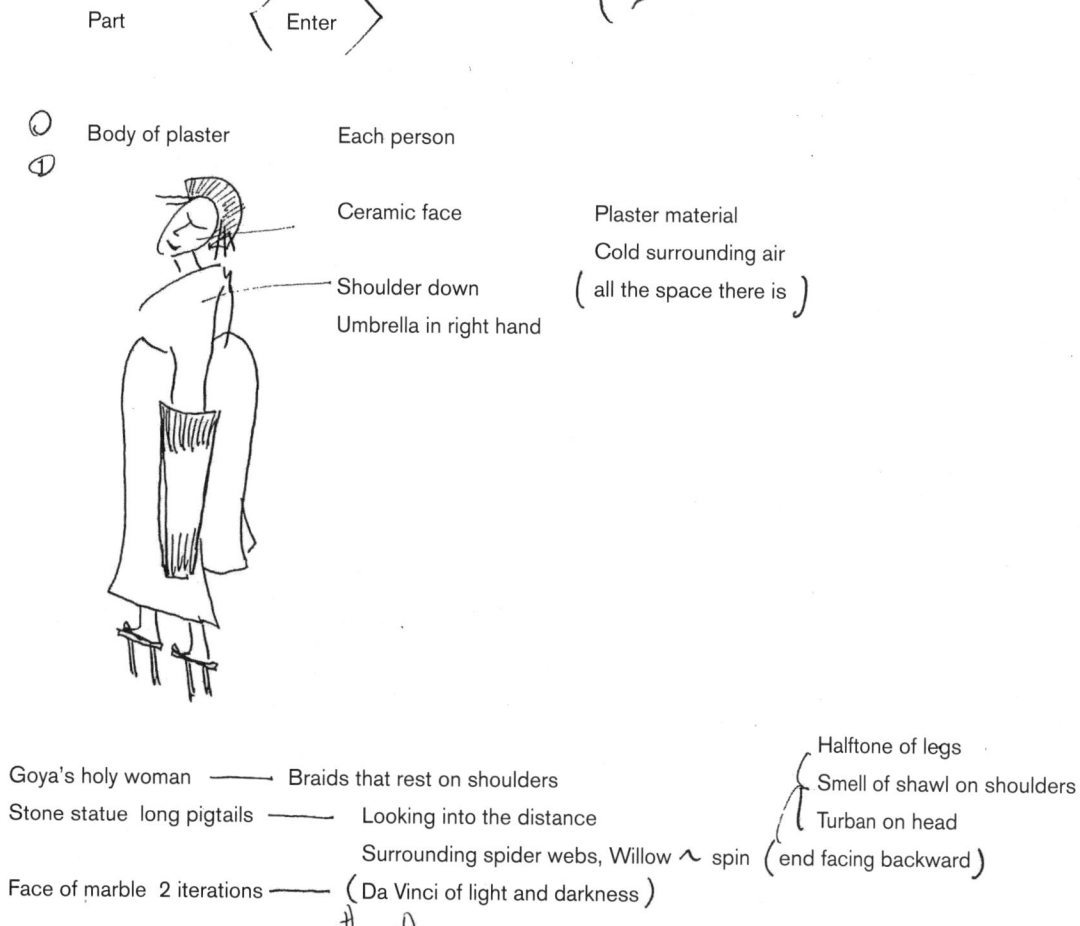

                                                                 Halftone of legs
② Goya's holy woman ——— Braids that rest on shoulders   Smell of shawl on shoulders
③ Stone statue long pigtails ——— Looking into the distance   Turban on head
                                 Surrounding spider webs, Willow ∼ spin (end facing backward)
④ Face of marble 2 iterations ——— (Da Vinci of light and darkness)

⑤ Paolo   ——— (Light and darkness
⑥ Directly in front ___   (Light and darkness   ⟩ without sitting
                               (White lion

○　アラー　　　（祈る白衣）　　　　　B

左肩上げる
［…］ひく

○　座る神様　　（振れる神様）

① 振れる神様 ┤a. 左手の一本指
　　　　　　　└b. 前のめりの手

② 振れる神様 ┤a. 〃
　　　　　　　└b. うす笑いの神様　（右
　　　　　── ヤリ ── 座ったまま飛ぶ

③　とうもろこし　　ヒゲとの間で振れている

④　ザクロかかげつ照りとかげり
　　　　毛細血管

○   Allah   (White prayer gown)   B

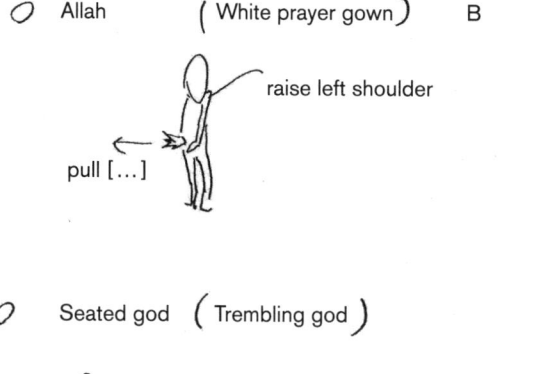

raise left shoulder

pull [...]

○   Seated god   (Trembling god)

① Trembling god ─┬─ a. Single finger on left hand
                 └─ b. Hand leaning forward

② Trembling god ─┬─ a. ″
                 └─ b. Lightly laughing god (right
                 ── Spear ── Leap while sitting

③ Corn   shaking between itself and beard

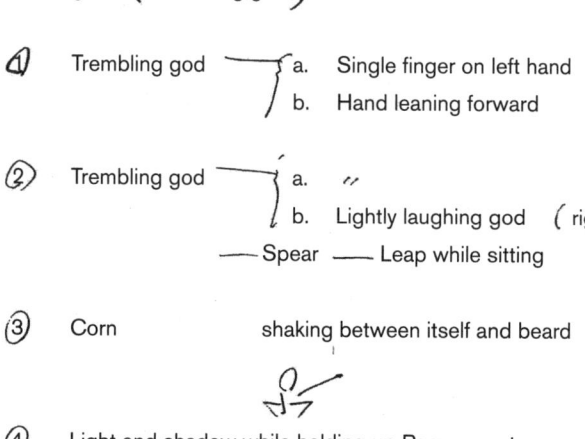

④ Light and shadow while holding up Pomegranate
    Capillary

クレンチ
0　空洞の馬

　ホートリエ　〜森の中、馬　①
　　　　　　（そのまま下る）　②
　　　　　　（左肩下げ）　　　③

0　石の鳥　　　　　　　ホートリエの材質 — 素の顔 — 石の原質 ｛すすける／粒子

　横向き、手前右を見る　　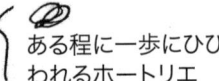 ある程に一歩にひび
　　　　　　　　　　　　　　　　　われるホートリエ

0　馬の首ホートリエ

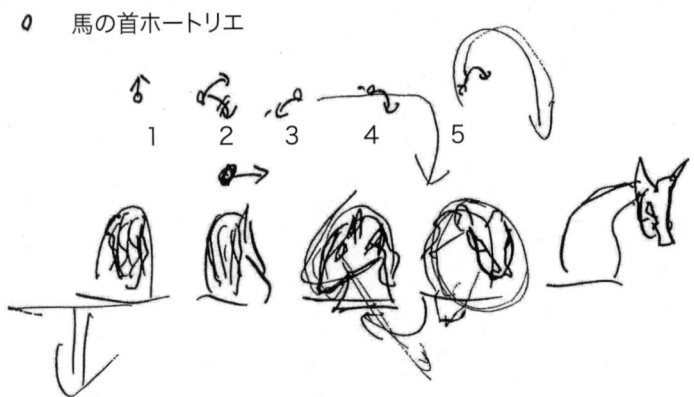

CLENCH

◦ Horse in a cavern

Fautrier   ~   In the woods, horse ①
(go down as is) ″ ②
(left shoulder down) ③

◦ Bird of stone   Fautrier's materials — Natural face — Essence of stone { Grow soot-covered Particle

Facing sideways, look at front right   { Fautrier cracked by a single step — to a degree

◦ Horse neck Fautrier

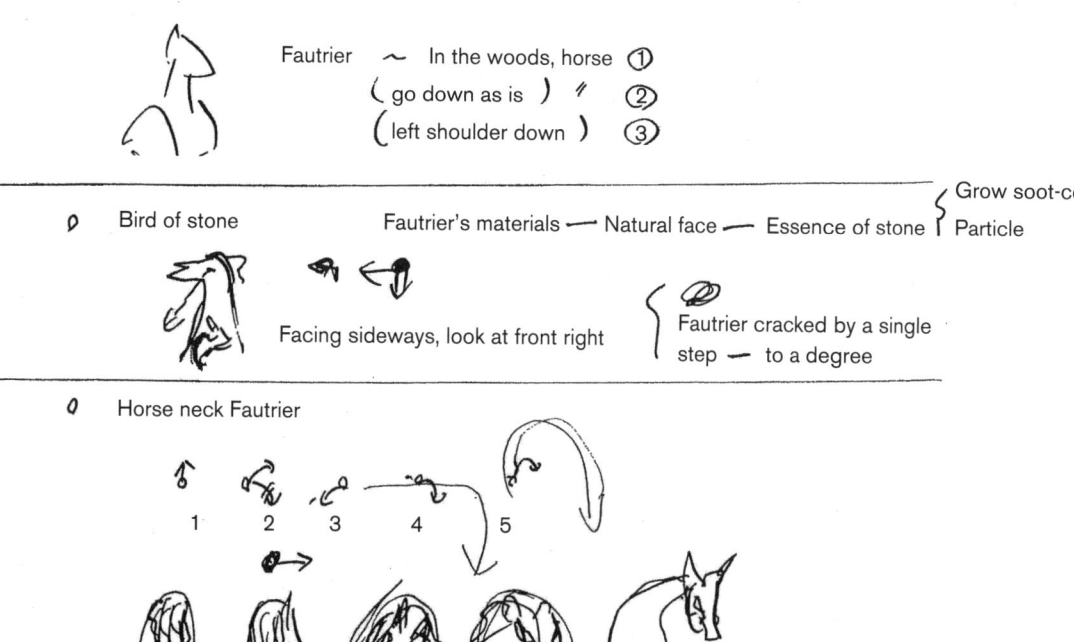

部分　(各人使用)

｛ 泣く女で座っている
　 五月の花むこ　　　(虫噛いがほうけてしまった)
　 ハンカチ　　　　　ゴヤ体は全部体の中でやる
　 ゴヤの銀の針状の怪物　羽がフアと上る途中

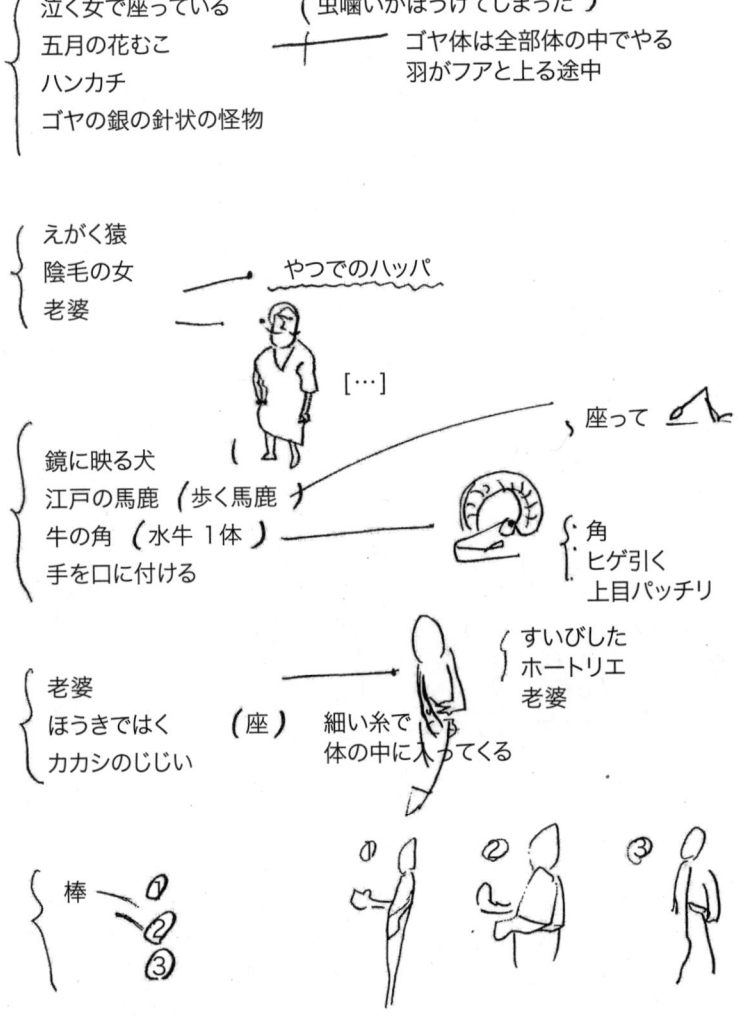

｛ えがく猿
　 陰毛の女　　　やつでのハッパ
　 老婆

　　　　　　　　　　　　　　座って

｛ 鏡に映る犬
　 江戸の馬鹿 (歩く馬鹿)
　 牛の角 (水牛 1体)　　　　｛ 角
　 手を口に付ける　　　　　　 ヒゲ引く
　　　　　　　　　　　　　　　上目パッチリ

　　　　　　　　　　　　　　｛ すいびした
｛ 老婆　　　　　　　　　　　 ホートリエ
　 ほうきではく　(座)　細い糸で　老婆
　 カカシのじじい　　　体の中に入ってくる

｛ 棒

Part (used by each person)

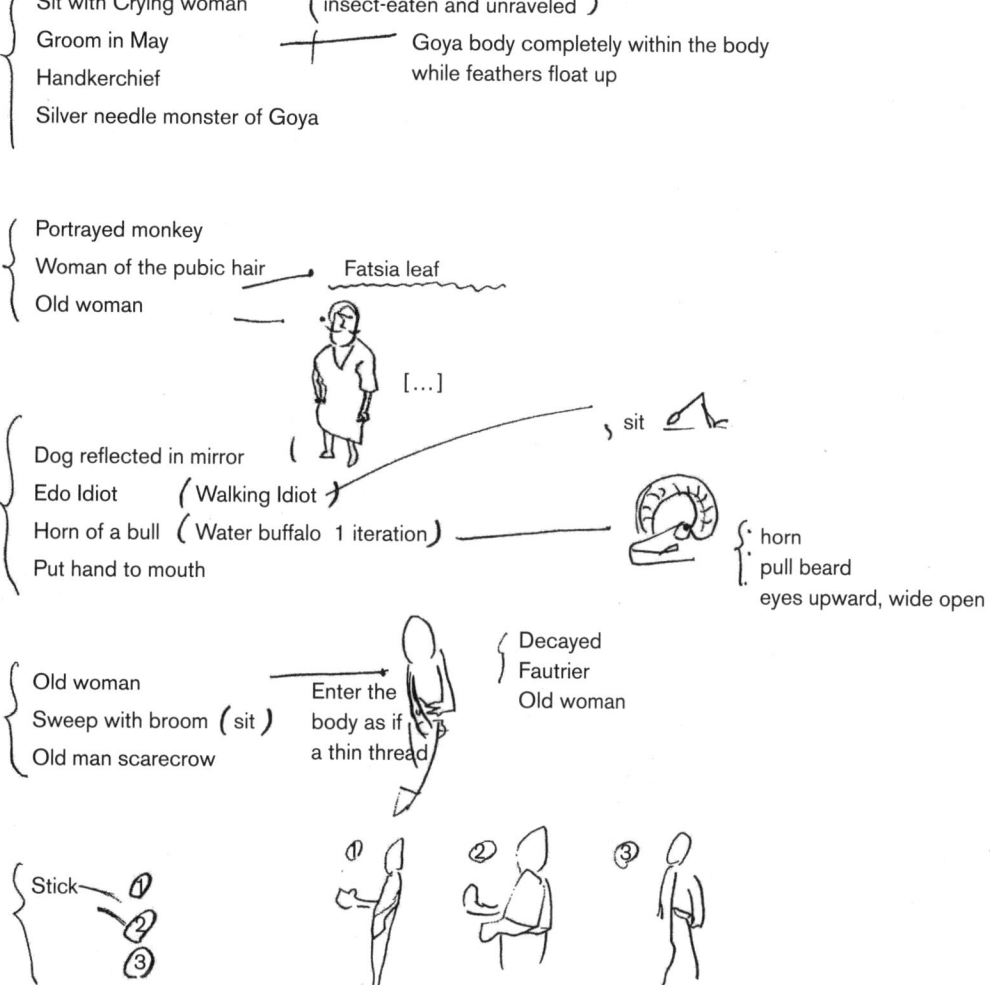

{ Sit with Crying woman (insect-eaten and unraveled)
  Groom in May ——— Goya body completely within the body
  Handkerchief   while feathers float up
  Silver needle monster of Goya

{ Portrayed monkey
  Woman of the pubic hair • Fatsia leaf
  Old woman

[…]

, sit

{ Dog reflected in mirror
  Edo Idiot   (Walking Idiot)
  Horn of a bull (Water buffalo 1 iteration) ———
  Put hand to mouth

{ horn
  pull beard
  eyes upward, wide open

{ Decayed
  Fautrier
  Old woman

{ Old woman
  Sweep with broom (sit)   Enter the body as if a thin thread
  Old man scarecrow

{ Stick — ①
         ②
         ③

① ② ③

〈 最後 ― ラストシーン 〉

せっこうの顔で板付

座 { キバ鬼空間と三ツ目鬼空間　　　〜 さらし首
　　ギガク面のみ　　　　　　　　　　1つずつ尻の羽（フワァ〜）
　　森の中の顔のくらやみ

{ 鳥　（横向き、細い石の鳥）　〜 フカン
　花鳥図　　　2回　　　途中パウロ
　ウランギーラ

{ 石像体

{ キバ鬼　　空間の毛空間
　ゴヤの怪人　（何体かやりながら座す）
　白い光馬　　（立とうとするトイエン）

　　　　　　　　　　　　　　　{ 化面の森
　　　　　　　　　　　　　　　　動かないすすける

クレンチの馬
{ ホートリエ　　空洞の馬
　　　　　　　髪の毛の座った馬より　3体

{ マヌカンで立つ　　　　→
　ピカソのハンカチ

{ 座って
　蛇

⟨ End —— Last Scene ⟩

In place when curtains open, with Plaster face

Sit {
  Space of fanged demons and Space of three-eyed demons ∼ Pilloried neck
  Only Gigaku masks —————— Buttock feathers, one at a time (*fuwaa* [lightly])
  Darkness of the face in the woods
}

{
  Bird (facing sideways, bird of thin stone) ∼ View from above
  Bird and flower painting   2 times   Paolo midway
  […]
}

{ Stone statue body

{
  Fanged demon   Hair Space in the space
  Goya's phantom   (Sit while doing several iterations)
  Horse of white light (Toyen trying to stand)
}

                                              (forest of Masks
                                                 immobile and blackened
Horse of Clench { Fautrier   Horse in cavern
                         3 iterations from the horses with seated hair

{
  Stand with Mannequin   ⟶
  Picasso's handkerchief
}

{
  Sit
  Snake
}

ようこうろ、風の音　　　————　金魚鉢のわれる音

　｛清姫
　　沼の重い顔で沈む
　　すすける

　｛かんかくの立体化

　柳空間　　｛つるぎ
　　　　　　玉を持つコロコロ　　｝密教
　　　　　　合掌
　　　　　｛くり返し

　空気する柳
　もうろうとする
　セッコウ

Furnace, sound of wind ———— Sound of goldfish bowl breaking

{ Kiyohime [snake princess]   Paolo

Sink with heavy swamp face

Get sooty

(Sensation goes three-dimensional   ↓↓↓

Willow Space   { Sword
Holding a ball *koro koro* [rolling]   } Esoteric Buddhism
Hands together in prayer

{ Repeat

Willow doing air
In a hazy stupor
Plaster

ψ

（子供）

— 花の中の少女　　A
　　　　　　　　　B
— ファ〜と立ち上り
— 野花空間　（アクリル空間）—— 凸凹の移動

— ~~ソロモン王宮~~　　ベーコン

(CHILD)

— Girl in the flowers A
　　　　　　　　　　B
— Stand up *fuaaa* [with a light air]
— Wildflower Space (Acrylic Space) —— unevenness in changing location

— ~~Court of Solomon~~　　Bacon

[藤の野・解剖図鑑]

- 馬鹿 ｛ 子供12相
　　　　　ピアズレパーティー　狂人パーティ

- 鯨線の各人の出だし
　　2回目の出より　　　　　　　孔雀心理

金魚 ｛ ― 和栗デュエット用ソロ　…‥　まわり神経によって孔雀続ける
　　　 ― 山本ラッパ
　　　 ― 立ってさがる　　　　→ ふかん孔雀（移動）
　　　　　　　　　　　　　　　　　小山人物交換
　　　　　　　　　　　　　　　　　山本を追い出す

　　　｛ ― 雨宮ソロ
　　　　 ― 孔雀シッポそろえて　→ 立って台の上

　　　（山本　　白チューリップ）　○新人　| 扇の出 |

- 浅田が入る

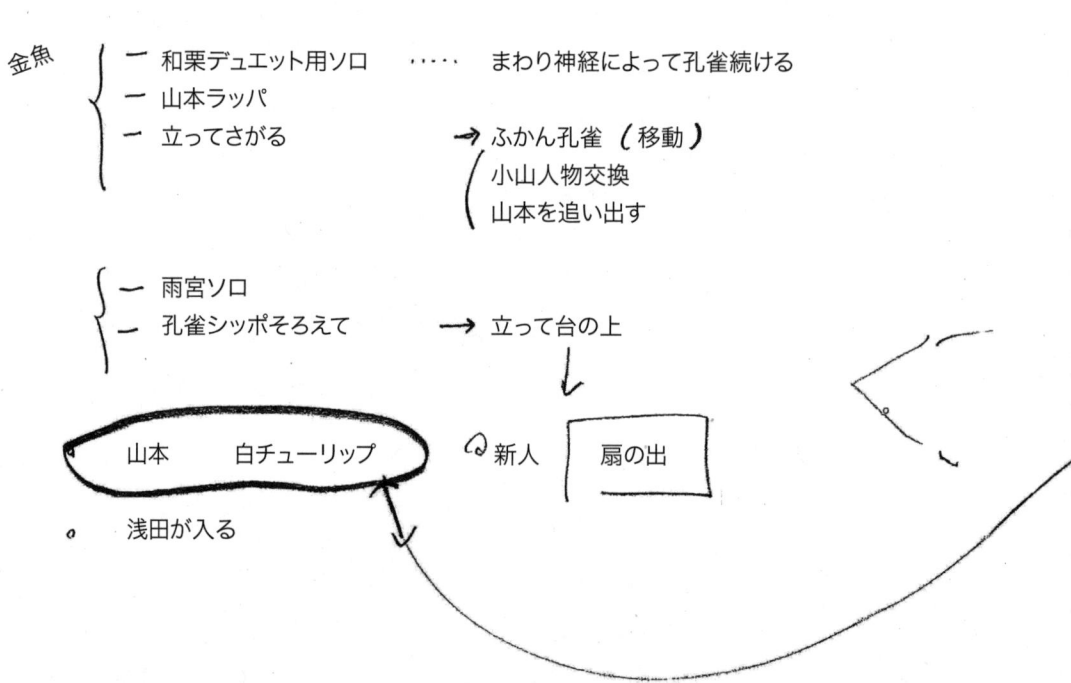

[金魚鉢]

っ 最後全員フィナーレ

[*FUJI NO NO* – Anatomical Picture Book]

- Idiot ⎧ Set of 12 child movements
  ⎩ Beardsley party   Lunatic party

- Each person's opening part for Whale Strings
  From the second entrance   Peacock psychology

Goldfish ⎧ — Solo for WAGURI duet ···· Continue peacock according to surrounding nerves
⎨ — YAMAMOTO bugle
⎩ — Stand and go back   → Peacock looks from above *(relocate)*
                              Koyama change characters
                              chase out YAMAMOTO

⎧ — AMAMIYA solo
⎩ — Peacocks line up their tails ⟶ stand up on the platform

(YAMAMOTO   White Tulip)   ⟲ Newcomer | enter with Fan

- ASADA enters

[GOLDFISH BOWL]

♪ Finale with all

● < 黒ドレス >　　41

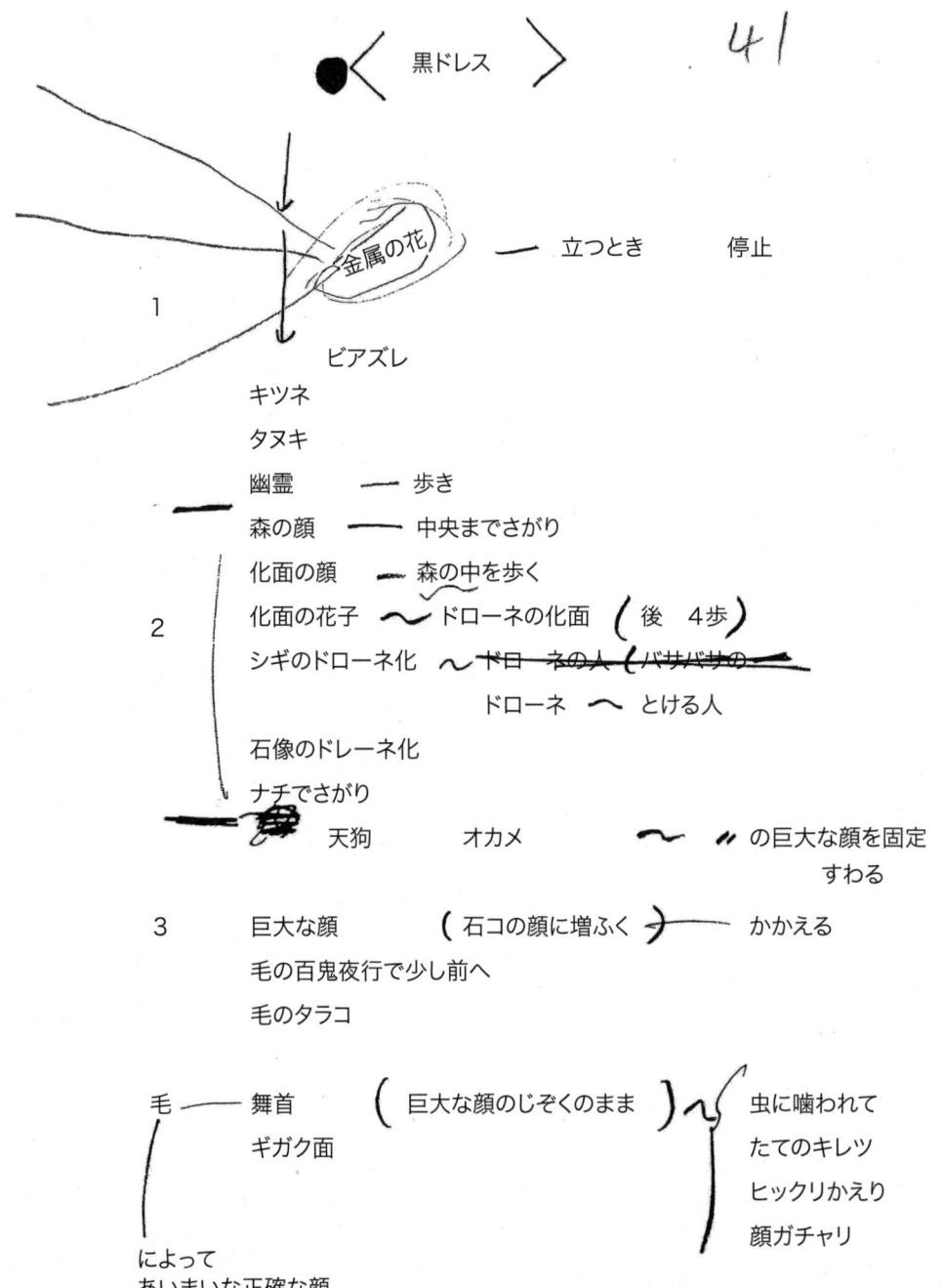

1　　金属の花　　— 立つとき　　停止

　　　　　ピアズレ
　　　キツネ
　　　タヌキ
　—　幽霊　　— 歩き
　　　森の顔　— 中央までさがり
　　　化面の顔　— 森の中を歩く
2　　化面の花子　〜 ドローネの化面（後　4歩）
　　　シギのドローネ化　〜ドローネの人（バサバサの
　　　　　　　　　　　ドローネ　〜　とける人

　　　石像のドレーネ化
　　　ナチでさがり
　　　　　　　天狗　　　オカメ　　〜　〃 の巨大な顔を固定
　　　　　　　　　　　　　　　　　　　　　すわる

3　　巨大な顔　　（石コの顔に増ふく ）— かかえる
　　　毛の百鬼夜行で少し前へ
　　　毛のタラコ

　毛 — 舞首　　（巨大な顔のじぞくのまま ）虫に噛まれて
　　　ギガク面　　　　　　　　　　　　　　たてのキレツ
　　　　　　　　　　　　　　　　　　　　　ヒックリかえり
　　　　　　　　　　　　　　　　　　　　　顔ガチャリ
　によって
　あいまいな正確な顔

⚫ ⟨ BLACK DRESS ⟩ 41

Metallic flowers — when standing   pause

1

Beardsley

Fox

Raccoon dog

Ghost — walk

Face in the woods — go back to the center

Face of the mask — walk through the woods

2   Hanako with mask ~ Delaunay's mask (back 4 steps)

Delaunay-ization of the sandpiper ~ ~~Delaunay's people~~ (~~basabasa~~

Delaunay ⌒ Melting person

Delaunay-ization of the stone statue

Go down with Nazi

Fix the Gigantic faces of   Tengu   Okame ~ "

sit

3   Gigantic face   (amplify on plaster face) — carry

A little forward with the Hyakki Yagyō of hair

Tarako of hair

Hair — Maikubi   (while sustaining the Gigantic faces)   Insect-eaten

Gigaku masks   Vertical break

Turned upside down

Face is *gachari* [crashed]

because of it,
ambiguously correct face

　　　　　　　　　（死の […] 水 → ビニール）をひっぱり前へ
　―　　　― 落下　　　― 人形の手

　　　4　　トリスタンで引いて
　　　　　　― 流れ首　　　← ホートリエ
　　　　　　― ドローネの逆でひいてきて「とける人
　　　　　　― 沼
　　　　　　― タヌキ 、幽霊
　　　　　　― コブ　　 〜 コン棒でさがり
　　　　　　― 合掌で↗で出て
　　　　　　― キバ 鬼空間 で
　　　　　　― 三ツ目 キバ 空間 でさがり
　　　　　　― 天狗オカメ 空間 でさらにさがる
　　　　　　― 巨大化したまま

　　　　　　〜 スカートを持ち上げる

　　　　回るスカート ｛ ガイコツ
　　　　　　　　　　　　　　　　　後ろ髪の毛
　　　　　　　　　　　　　　　　　首すじ
　　　　　　　　　　　　　　　　　形とり
　　　　　　　　　　　　　　　　　斜めのひきつり

　　　　　― ギガク面

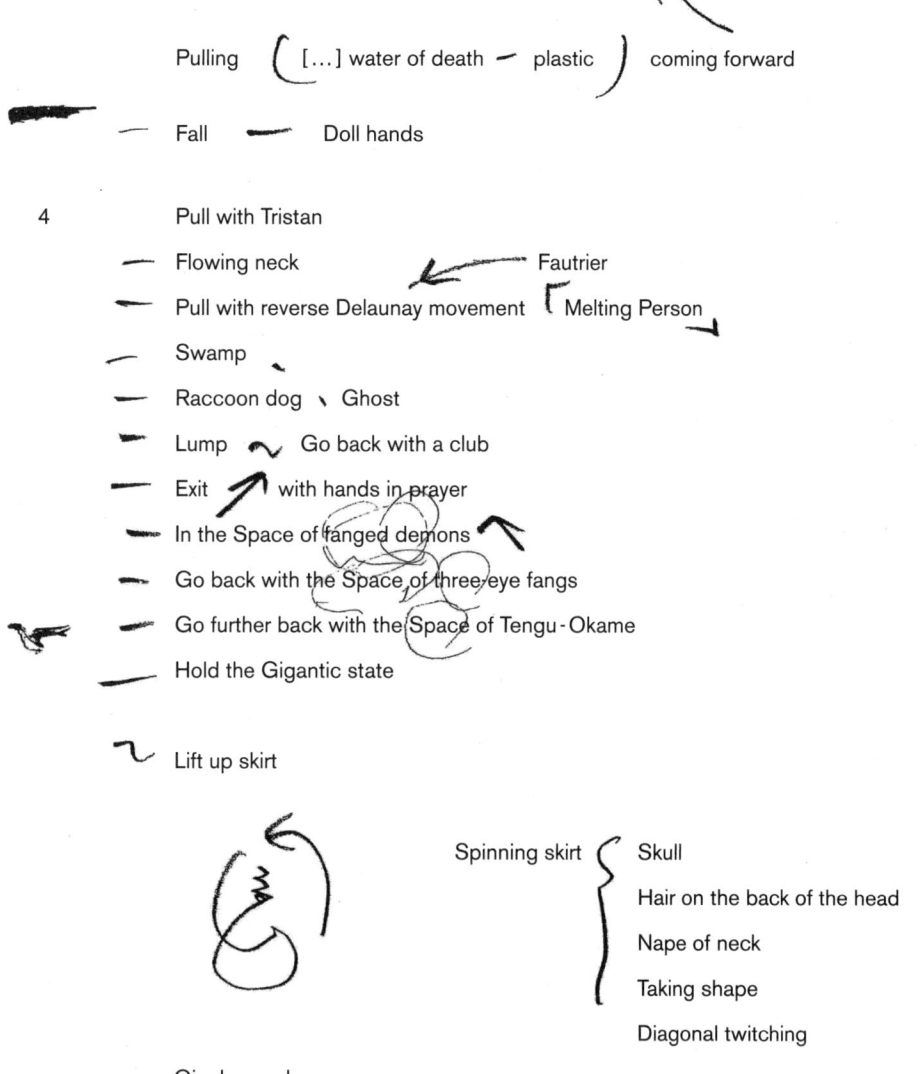

Pulling ([...] water of death — plastic) coming forward

— Fall — Doll hands

4 Pull with Tristan
— Flowing neck   Fautrier
— Pull with reverse Delaunay movement Melting Person
— Swamp
— Raccoon dog \ Ghost
— Lump Go back with a club
— Exit with hands in prayer
— In the Space of fanged demons
— Go back with the Space of three-eye fangs
— Go further back with the Space of Tengu-Okame
— Hold the Gigantic state

Lift up skirt

Spinning skirt { Skull
Hair on the back of the head
Nape of neck
Taking shape
Diagonal twitching

— Gigaku masks

ラッパ　トレスより（切レ目）　　　　　　　　｝コミカル
ライトに入り　正面ラッパ　3回繰り返す

　｜前と同じ
───────────────────────────────────────

光の人物体　　｛背ズイカリエス
　　　　　　　　箱
　　　　　　　　両手に光
　　　　　　　　死に首
　　　　　　　　オルフェー

ハスを取りながら
中腰の低迷より

ビアズレの人物

　　　　　　　｛センスを持った人（せっぷん天使）
　　　　　　　　下を見る人
　　　　　　　　馬の首　〜　微笑
　　　　　　　　なんでもない人
　　　　　　　　祈のり
　　　　　　　　ヒゲの長い人　　　　　｛フカンされ
　　　　　　　　　　　　　　　　　　　　銀のハリの人物4体
トイエンで立ってゆく　　　　　　　　　　炎の人

───────────────────────────────────────

病んだ少年の顔　　　　　　　　　　　　　　　｝カイキ
ナチの顔　　〜　ヒゲに関わり
ガイコツを据える
玉を持つ　　〜　顔でわり
甲中
（体をおこして（ホトリエの材質を見せるだけ）

Bugle   from tracing paper (a tear)   ⎞
Enter the light   Bugle en face   repeat 3 times   ⎟ comical
                                                          ⎠
       | same as before

Body of person in light ⎧ Spinal decay
                         ⎪ Box
                         ⎨ Light in both hands
                         ⎪ Dying neck
                         ⎩ Orpheus

   While taking the lotus
   with a half-crouched stagnation

Beardsley's characters
                         ⎧ Person holding fan (Kissing angel)
                         ⎪ Person looking down
                         ⎨ Horse neck ∼ Slight smile
                         ⎪ Ordinary person
                         ⎪ Prayer
                         ⎩ Person with long beard ──────┐   ⎧ Viewed from above
                                                       ⎨ Silver needle people 4 iterations
Stand and go with Toyen   ⎩ Flame person

Face of sick young boy   ⎞
Face of Nazis ∼ engaging the beard   ⎟
Fix a skull in place   ⎟ bizarre
Hold a ball ∼ split with the face   ⎟
Inside the armor   ⎟
(Raising the body (only to show Fautrier's materials) ⎠

1. 門達 –– 金魚のヒラヒラ
   a. サイの分かつの時 〈 ウラで運び / 途中赤チラチラ 〉 またがる
   b. 藤野花

↓

〈そう入〉
1. 門
2. 藤野
3. 剛直
4. 浅
｝柱

– 手を下し、回る（へき面）
　　– 長く ⟶ 山本入る
– 手に戻る — めいめいの場所へ
– 手の動きの残り –– すぐひっこみ

・照明（アンバー … サイ
　　　　薄いブルー
・暗黒 … のたれ幕 … 寮より持ってくる
・舞台の黒ペンキ
・金パクのツカケ　　・ヤリ
・スライド直し　　　・最後スライド
・ニカワのそで　　　・フック

・虹の衣裳 –– 黒布買う　ぬう

・カミソリ –– ペーパー
・棒（丸たん棒）4本（鉄砲）
・~~アラの背中のスタンプ~~ … バラ
・門 ––（金魚）そでをもらう
　　　　　　ヒラヒラ
　門達 –– 頭ずきんする（白）

・ソロモン王宮 –– 金カク寺
　　　　　　　全員付ける（五人）

2. 太陽のキラキラ　　　金魚鉢
   a. 門 –– 中
      （ニ –– 上・下）板付き
   b. – 剛直、晴三 さがり
      – 五人組交互に 三人と交差するように
      ↓　　　三人の着替えの時間かせぐ

   全員ブルーの衣裳でラスト

   動き　　パネル
   　　　　　三
   サイ – 頭　　　　　　　　　　　　　） 1
   　　　　　　　分れつ
   　　 – シッポ
   　　 – 頭とシッポ　合体　　　　　　） 2
   　　 – 頭シッポ　開き　　胴入り
   　　 – (左おれる（うしろ）
   　　 胴　前に　　　　　　　　　) 3
   　　 頭
   　　 – バラバラに　横に　　　　　　 4
   　　 – 歩る　交差して歩る　　　　　 5
   　　 – 〃　　　　　　　　　　　　　 6
   　　 – まちがえて　パネル

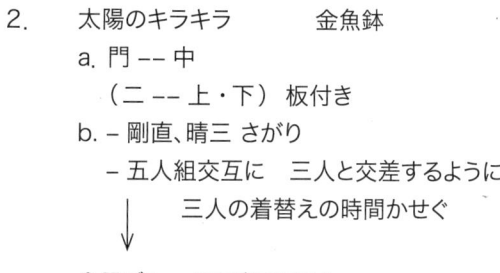

3. ピンクの帽子の追加　サイの場面にそう入

4. デュエット・クシの場面
   　　　・浅田 –– 台の上
   　　　・（門・剛直の –– 台下）

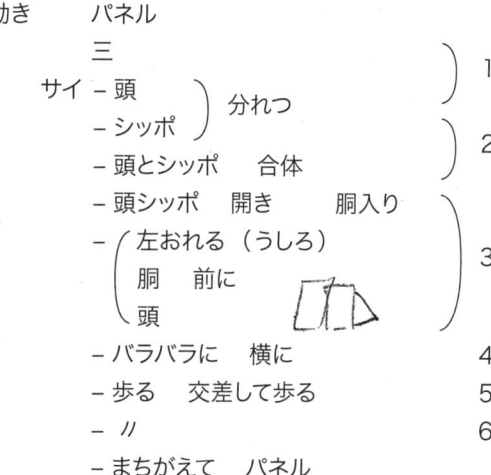

   カブ –– 浅田
   ゴヤ –– 2人
   　　二人交差
   　　　│
   　　二人　　ひきつり　台にさがり　F.O.
   前、途中一人で踊ることになるかもしれない

1.   MON et al —— Fluttering goldfish fins
   a. When rhinoceroses branch off ⟨ Carry backstage
   b. FUJINO flowers   Little flashes   ⟩ Straddle
                               of red midway

⟨ Insert ⟩ ↓
1. MON ⎫
2. FUJINO ⎬ Column
3. GŌCHOKU ⎪
4. ASA ⎭

    — Lower hand, spin (Wall surface)
       — Long ⟶ YAMAMOTO enters
    — Return to hand —— each to their spot
    — ~~Remainder~~ of hand movement —— retract quickly

- Lighting ⎛ Amber   … Rhinoceros
             ⎝ Light blue

- Darkness … Drop curtain … bring from the dormitory
- Black paint on the stage
- Gold leaf mechanism   • Spear
- Fix slides   • Final slide
- *Nikawa* [glue] sleeves   • Hook

- ~~Rainbow costume~~ —— buy black cloth, sew

- Razor —— Paper
- Stick (club)   4 (guns)
- ~~Stamp on Allah's back~~ … Roses
- MON —— (Goldfish) receive the sleeve
                fluttering
   MON et al —— Put on a hood (white)

- Court of Solomon —— Temple of the Golden Pavilion (hat)
                     Everyone put it on (5 people)

2.   Sparkle of the sun   Goldfish bowl

    a. MON —— in the center

       (Two —— Up Down)   Dancers in place when curtain rises

    b. — GŌCHOKU, SEIZŌ go back

       — Groups of five alternating   make three people intersect

          ↓   Buy time for three people to change costumes

All in blue costumes for the final scene

    Movement   Panel

              Three

    Rhinoceros — Head ⎞   ⎞ 1

           — Tail   ⎠ division

                                                ⎠ 2

           — Head and tail merge

           — Headtail open   Torso enters

           — ⎛ Left panel breaks (falls back)

              ⎜ Torso front   ⎠ 3

              ⎝ Head

           — In pieces to the side   4

           — Run   run and intersect   5

           —   "   6

           — Panel moves by mistake

3.   Passage of pink hat   Insert into rhinoceros scene

4.   Duet • Comb Scene

        • ASADA —— on platform

        • (MON, GŌCHOKU —— below platform)

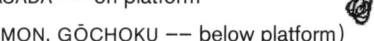

Gabu —— ASADA

Goya —— 2 people

    Two people intersect

       |

    Two people   twitching   return to platform F.O.

    Front, might end up dancing alone midway

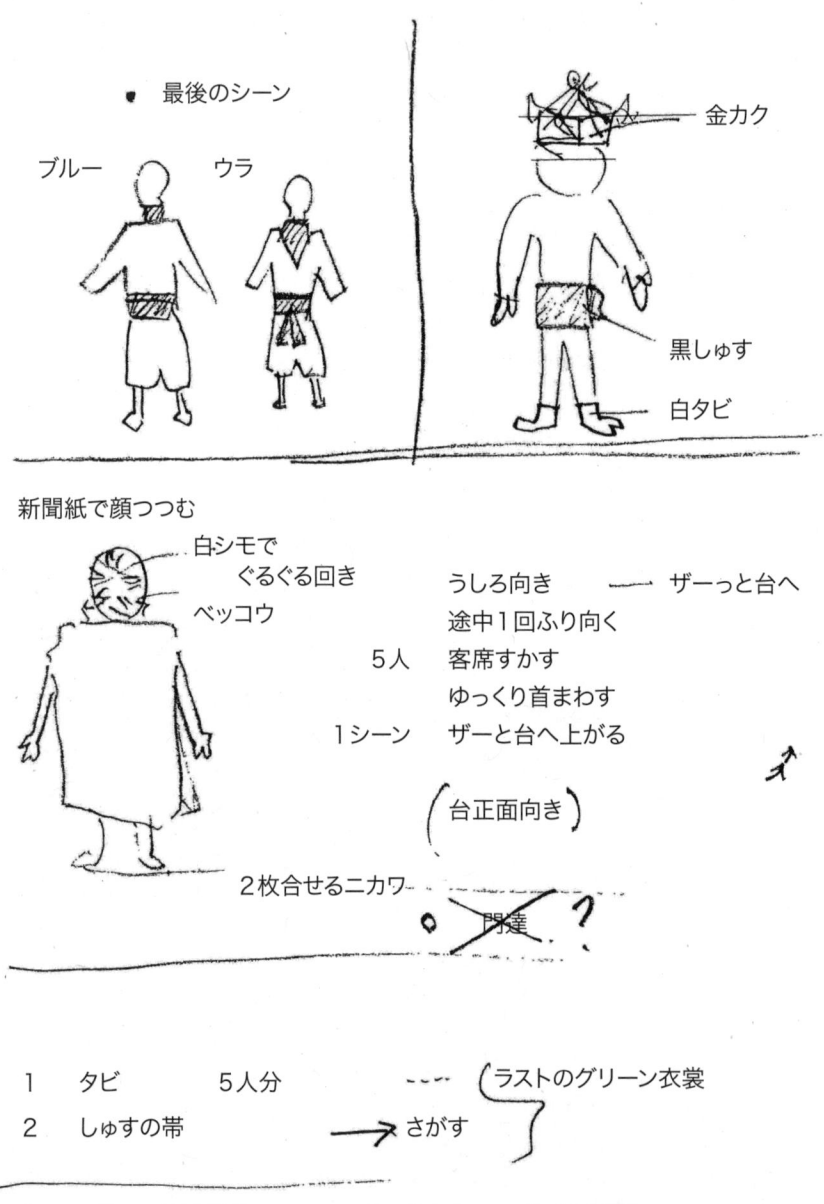

1　タビ　　　5人分　　　　------ ラストのグリーン衣裳
2　しゅすの帯　　　→　さがす

3.　ニカワの甲中製作　→　3人分 ＼＼ サイの場面

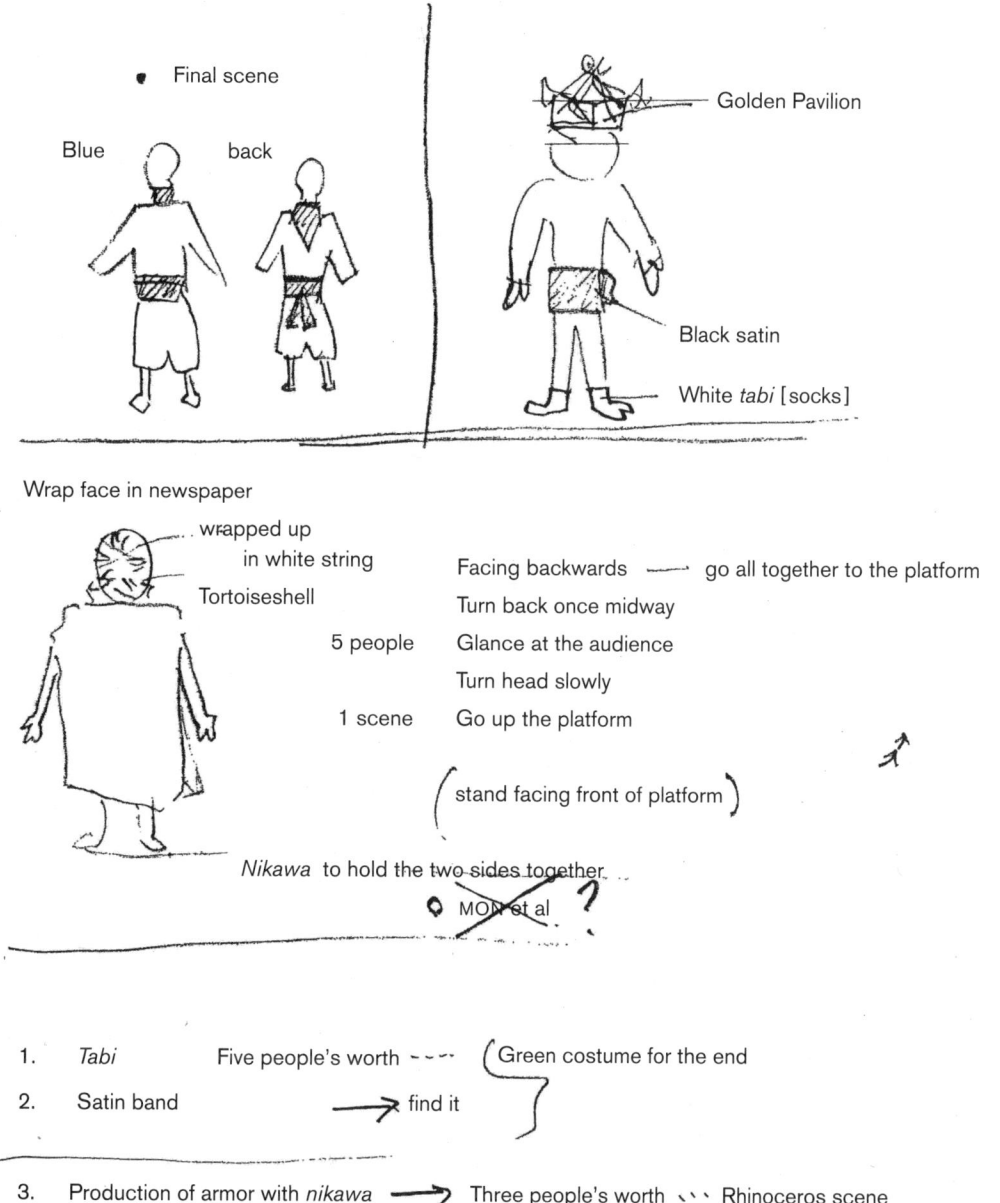

Final scene

Blue   back

Golden Pavilion

Black satin

White *tabi* [socks]

Wrap face in newspaper

wrapped up in white string

Tortoiseshell

5 people

1 scene

Facing backwards ⎯⎯ go all together to the platform
Turn back once midway
Glance at the audience
Turn head slowly
Go up the platform

(stand facing front of platform)

Nikawa to hold the two sides together

1. *Tabi*   Five people's worth --- ⎫ Green costume for the end
2. Satin band   ⎯→ find it   ⎭

3. Production of armor with *nikawa* ⎯→ Three people's worth ⟍⟍ Rhinoceros scene

・黒ドレス（下手より）――ヤリに首をさされた魔女
魔女の登場
　　　　　　　　　――金属の花途中 停止
　　　　　　　　　――人形の手
　　　　　　　　　――化面
　　　　　　　　　――ギガク面より舞首⇔鬼の百鬼夜行
　　　　　　　　　――流れ首 停止

・子供（台上）　沼　深海

A・金魚（装置転換と同時）

B・裸体（馬の役）――甲中と同じ出　水中
　　　　　　　　――人魚に3回合図

C・金魚

・心理（各人の出）

・グリーン（台上正面）

・白ドレス（正面）――石像――死んで石に変質してゆくプロセス
　　　　　　　　　――聖少女の髪の毛――バリの怪人
　　　　　　　　　――セッコウの手
　　　　　　　　　　センス　　　　――キツネ空間

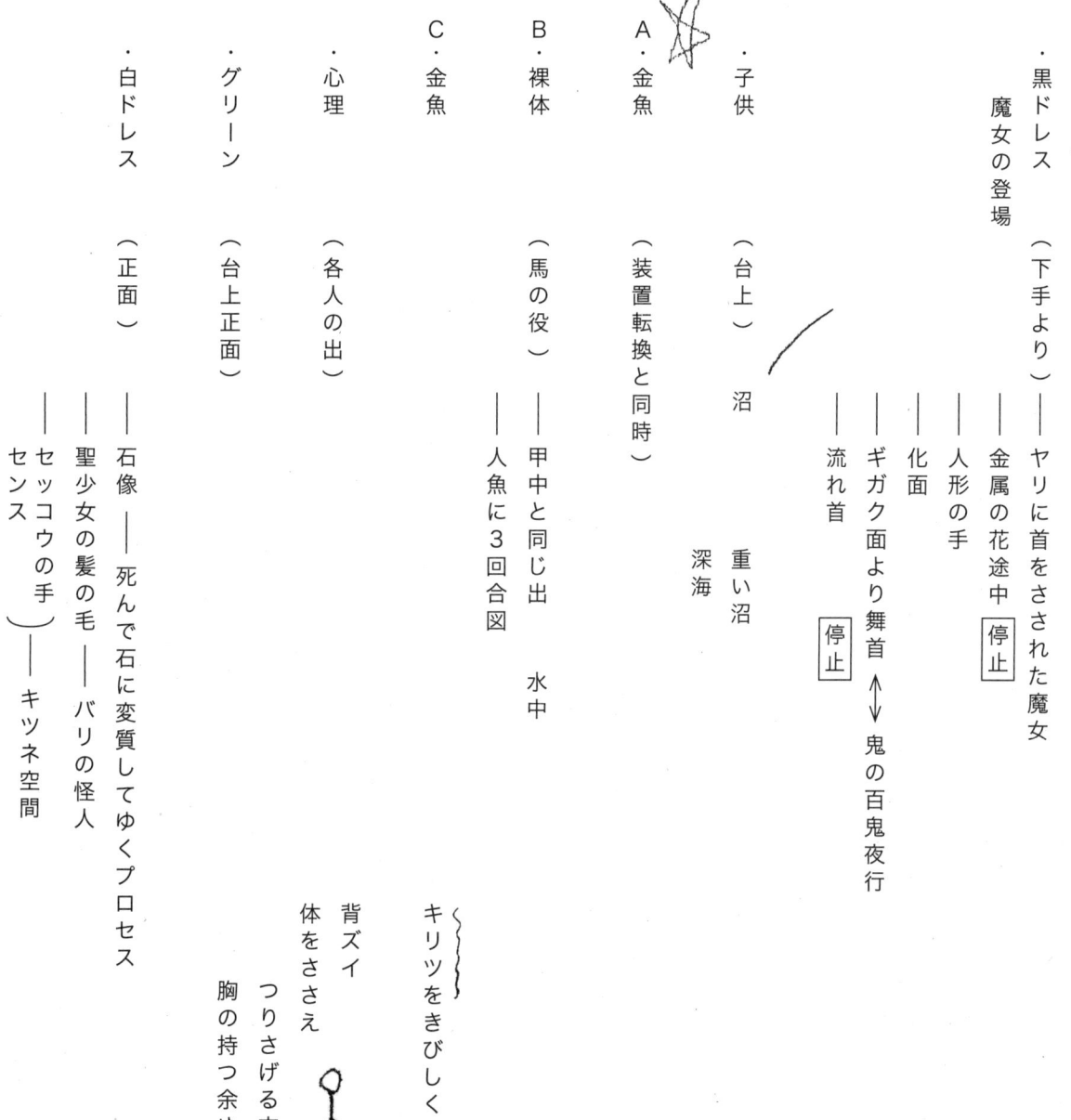

キリツをきびしく
背ズイ
体をささえ　つりさげる支点
胸の持つ余ゆう

- **BLACK DRESS** (from stage right) —— Witch struck by a spear
  Witch enters —— Metallic flowers midway [Pause]
  —— Doll hands
  —— Mask
  —— Maikubi from Gigaku masks ⟺ Hyakki Yagyō
  —— Flowing neck [Pause]

- **CHILD** (on platform) Swamp Heavy swamp
  Deep ocean

A • **GOLDFISH** (same time as set change)

B • **NAKED BODY** (Horse role) —— Same entry as inside the armor (underwater)
  —— 3 signals to the mermaid

C • **GOLDFISH**

  Stand up strictly

- **PSYCHOLOGY** (each person enters)
  Spinal cord
  Support the body
  Supporting point for suspension
  Breathing room of the heart

- **GREEN** (on platform facing front)

- **WHITE DRESS** (facing front) —— Stone sculpture —— Process of dying and turning to stone
  —— Hair of the holy young girl —— Phantom of Bali
  —— Plaster hand
  Folding fan }— Fox Space

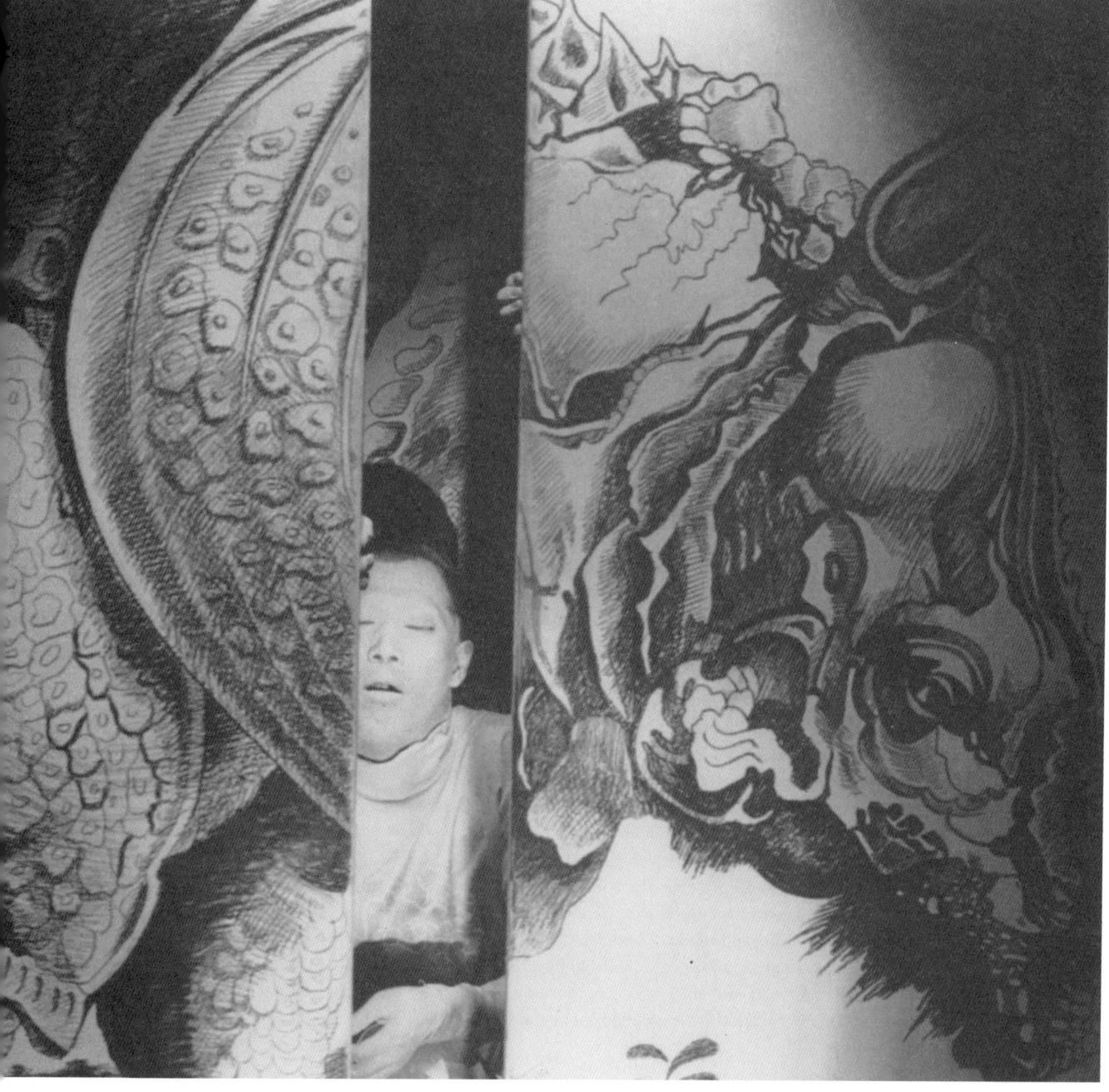

SHŌMEN NO ISHŌ (COSTUME EN FACE):
BUTOH IN 1976

TAKASHI MORISHITA

Adapted from "Method of 1976," in Morishita Takashi, Tatsumi Hijikata's Notational Butoh: Sign and Method for Creation, Keio University Art Center, 2010.

From 1974 to 1976, a series of Hakutōbō performances was going on at Tatsumi Hijikata's Asbestos-studio, during which Hijikata created and presented 16 works. The Butoh dance with its strange title *Shōmen no ishō* [Costume en Face] was part of this extraordinary output of works. In 1976, *Hitogata* [Human Shape] and *Geisen jō no okugata* [Madame on Whale Strings], were performed with Yoko Ashikawa playing the leading role in both. *Costume en Face* was performed in October-November of the same year, and featured Moe Yamamoto in the leading role. For Yamamoto, this was the last piece he would perform for Hijikata before leaving Asbestos-studio and establishing his own Kanazawa Butoh-Kan.

Why did Hijikata create new works one after another, so intensively, in this two-year period? The significance of this enormous volume of works has not been analyzed, but it cannot be denied that the numerous serial performances were part of Hijikata's development of *'Butoh-fū'*, an original notation system for his Butoh. By the time *Costume en Face* was performed in 1976, Hijikata's notational Butoh was in its final stage of development.

Why do we turn to *Costume en Face* when considering Tatsumi Hijikata's notational Butoh? First, it is valuable in that it was created toward the end of Hijikata's experiments with notation, when Hijikata's notational Butoh was well developed. It is also unique in that the Butoh notes for the piece, written by Yamamoto, remain in their original notebook form. From the notebook notation, we can see the names of encoded 'movements' that were developed for the work, giving access to both the structure of the work and Hijikata's notational strategies. In addition, a video recording of the original stage performance is available (housed in the Hijikata Archive at Keio University) and the 'movements' can be compared between those physicalized in the video and those encoded in the notebook notation. This combination of resources is

COSTUME EN FACE
PERFORMANCE POSTER
(1976)

invaluable in understanding Hijikata's method of creating works and staging performances, and also analyzing his lexicon of images and artistic influences. Thus, *Costume en Face* is singular in its archival richness.

In 1976, when *Costume en Face* was performed, *Madame on Whale Strings* was the last Hakutōbō serial performance, presented in December. Described as *Ankoku Takarazuka* [Takarazuka of Darkness], *Madame on Whale Strings* turned out to be a mind-blowing show, with transcendent dancing by Yoko Ashikawa. In comparison with *Madame on Whale Strings*, although *Costume en Face* was relatively conservative, it was considered impressive due to its innovative scene changes, and because of the skilled dancing of the male performers and the fresh dancing of the young Yamamoto.

The serial performances were discontinued in 1976, perhaps a manifestation of entropy – that Hijikata's creative act had risen, reached its peak and burned out. Whether that meant the completion of Butoh based on *Butoh-fū* or not, we will consider below.

At that time Hijikata strove to physicalize 'movements' by stimulating the dancers' senses and nerves, rather than providing the 'movements' directly to the dancers' consciousness or reason. If dancers had hoped to dance on their own responsibility, it had to have been quite painful to respond to Hijikata's strict choreographic method. Yamamoto had no previous dance experience, and he devoted himself to dance training at Asbestos-studio for only two years. During those two years, Yamamoto played the key role only in *Costume en Face*. Otherwise, he danced as part of a chorus. Still, he took command of an excessive number of 'movements'. After two years, in order to continue dancing, he had to leave Asbestos-studio; Yamamoto has explained: "I was so filled with dances imparted by the teacher in those two years that I had to leave Asbestos-studio in order to see them objectively." [1]

Though Yamamoto's tenure at Asbestos-studio was relatively short, it was precisely that two-year period that saw such an extraordinary output of works. As I mentioned earlier, considering the sheer volume of material created, it must have been an absolute priority for Hijikata, imposed on himself, to generate a large amount of material through which he could develop a method of notational Butoh. In this respect, the year 1976, when the method of Butoh based on *Butoh-fū* was established, was an important one in Tatsumi Hijikata's Butoh. Below, I examine what constituted this 'method of 1976' (as I call it), both in terms of its methodology and its particular instantiation in *Costume en Face*.

A SCENE FROM
"COSTUME EN FACE"
(1976)

Butoh Notes, or Encoding

At Asbestos-studio, disciple/performers were required to carry a notebook when attending practice sessions and to record what Hijikata said, explained to them, and the particular phrases by which he instructed them. In addition to Hijikata's spoken words, the disciples wrote and sketched the images Hijikata showed them, along with anything else the disciple noticed during the sessions. Although the manner of taking notes was up to each disciple, Hijikata sometimes checked their notebooks and advised them on how to do so, or asked them to make modifications. In any case, nothing began without a notebook. Regardless of whether they were written down during practice sessions or added later, the words of Hijikata in instructing, prescribing or facilitating the movements of dancers were recorded. Yamamoto's notation for *Costume en Face* is one of these notebooks – 65 pages of a common B5-sized notebook. The notebook was obviously prepared exclusively for *Costume en Face* and for its performance. Let us open it now and consider what is distinctive about its contents.

The first thing to notice is that almost all the pages are filled with words of instruction on 'movements,' with illustrations here and there. Those must have been drawn based on images or photos Hijikata showed to Yamamoto as reference materials. Next, given that Yamamoto took notes for the purpose of performing the work,

STAGE MODEL OF ASBESTOS-STUDIO (1/10 SCALE, BY YOSHIE SHOZO)

we can see in the notebook the progression of movements and the structure formed through their combination. In other words, they were written according to scenes, with the names of 'movements' listed for each scene, according to the progressive composition of the work. Despite this careful process, some scenes in the notebook differ to various degrees from the actual stage performance because inevitably some sequences and movements were changed during later rehearsals.

This point should be particularly emphasized: these notes were mostly in 'code.' Each word can be understood to be the name of a 'movement,' but a third party could not know the actual movements created by Hijikata and then choreographed for Yamamoto. This alone means it is difficult to call the notes *'Butoh-fū.'* In order to understand *Butoh-fū* as a conventional notation or score, it should have either drawings to describe physical movements, or a score to show changes in time or space. In addition, there are no words to explain the theme or motif of *Costume en Face* as a work, or to describe its content or expressions. Sometimes these are explained through words that Hijikata used to prompt dancers (Yamamoto in this case) into thinking for their dancing, which enables us to imagine Butoh as Hijikata conceived of it. As a whole, however, it is a list of seemingly mechanical words and phrases.[2] Although I cannot tell from this exactly how much Hijikata explained the content of a work or his intention, I am sure at least that he didn't ask the dancers, his disciples, to understand the content or intention. What Hijikata demanded of them was that they physicalize 'movements' developed by him and acquire the skills for doing so.

Nevertheless, Yamamoto's notes are obviously very valuable as a means to consider and understand Butoh based on *Butoh-fū*. 'Movements' were not certain until words provided by Hijikata were embodied. And embodied 'movements' were recursively fixed in the form of words. This process was practiced and served as the core of creation/development of 'movements,' creating notation in the form of text. It goes without saying that this process does not cover everything in the creation/development of 'movements' – a separate process before Hijikata spoke his words – or the process in which a work was completed by being prompted by such fixed words. In any case, we may say that Yamamoto's body played a role in developing a solution to visualize 'movements,' and his body of notes, in which he devotedly recorded what Hijikata said, served to fix that solution and encode 'movements.'

Butoh Notes – Methods and Works

Let us look at the structure of Yamamoto's notes for *Costume en Face*. That structure is not exactly the same as his recorded performance of *Costume en Face*, but we can guess at the general structure and content. In his notes, Yamamoto recorded 'movements' of other dancers together with his own, but here I only focus on Yamamoto's 'movements.' First, titles of scenes in which Yamamoto played the main role are as follows:[3]

a. Old woman
b. Madame Beardsley
c. Angel blowing a bugle
d. Commander (Kaguya)
e. White dress (tulip)
f. Black dress
g. Psychology
h. Goldfish (rainbow costume)

Names of scenes seem to be described based on content or the characteristics of costumes. There are some without titles, which may suggest that there was no need for the performer to be concerned about the name of a scene or even its status as a scene. First, let us look at 'movements' in each scene [Table 1]:

Table 1: Scenes and 'Movements' in *Costume en Face*

Scene	Number of 'movements'	Number of names of 'movements'
Old woman	21	19
Madame Beardsley	37	40
Bugle angel	57	54
Commander	30	34
White dress	48	46
Black dress	63	62
Psychology 1	29	29
Psychology 2	28	32
Goldfish	43	45
TOTAL	356	337*

*This is not the total of 'movements' in each scene, but the total of 'movements' after subtracting those common throughout all scenes.

As can be seen from the table, in the scenes of *Costume en Face* in which Yamamoto performed, 356 'movements' were used – sometimes combinations of multiple movements. Counting the names of 'movements', we see there are 337 kinds of 'movements'. Depending on the scene, there are more names of 'movements' than actual 'movement' units. This is because a 'movement' combining multiple movements was also given a name.

In order for Yamamoto to perform *Costume en Face*, he had to master – that is, physicalize – at least 356 'movements'. More than 1,000 'movements' were identified in Yukio Waguri's *Butoh-fū*. In that sense, perhaps 300 cannot be said to be a lot. Yet clearly, 300 'movements', if one can freely dance them, means a work of great variety.

As Hijikata himself said: "One cannot dance even a bird in the true sense unless concentrating all one's nerves on the natural universe …"[4] Whether or not it is possible to "concentrate all one's nerves" when dancing a 'movement', Hijikata demanded that his dancers not simply imitate forms but rather achieved the much more severe and difficult task he set for them, regardless if these 'movements' numbered 300 or 1000.

Though the notebook notation does not grant us access to the meaning of the work itself or the intentions in Hijikata's expressions, we may nonetheless observe some characteristics from the names of the 'movements' in *Costume en Face*. Let us try to classify them [Table 2]:

Table 2: Characteristics from the Names of 'Movements' in *Costume en Face*

People	Madame Peacock, a plaster lady looking backward, Madame Boccaccio, the Pope of Brains, a holy woman
Animals	A raccoon dog, a fox, a cat, a peacock, a sea lion, a rhinoceros
Imaginary creatures	A ghost, a long-nosed goblin, a fanged demon, an angel (an angel of burns, a bugle angel, a kissing angel)
Abstracted creatures or bodies	A floating neck, a laughing berry, a melting person, a silver-needle person, a dismantling bird, a transformed chicken
Plants	A wildflower, a willow, a branching flower, a tulip
From paintings	Delaunay, Wols, Toyen, a child of Picasso, Madame Beardsley, Fautrier, Goya's phantom, Redon, a picture of flowers and birds
People in action	A person cutting grass, a woman in flames, a person repenting, a person playing *shōgi*, an old woman with a fan, a girl with flowers, a pianist
Faces embodying something	A face of a forest, a face of plaster, a woolly rhinoceros, a face in flames, a face of an insane person, a face of a sick boy, a face of a Nazi
Open spaces	Mirror space, plant space, swamp space, willow space, space of fanged demons, hair space
Figurative objects	An image of Kannon [goddess] with one thousand hands, a Gigaku mask, a plaster body, hairy cod roe
Actions	Holding a ball, sinking in a swamp with a heavy face, dislocation of hipbones, barking, diagonal twitching
Metaphysical	Understanding the feathers of a bugler, order of sea lions, horse of white light, a flower of meat, metallic flowers, stagnation of one hundred demons, dismantling one's gaze, willow doing air, making senses three-dimensional, Delaunay-ization of a stone statue

From the above table, there emerge certain characteristics: Hijikata repeatedly took up imaginary, grotesque creatures, including ghosts, long-nosed goblins and demons. He had male dancers perform a series of old women, including Madame Peacock, the plaster lady, and old woman with a fan. These characteristics constitute only a part of the 'movements' in *Costume en Face*. Overall, we can see Hijikata's intention to create/develop dances from a stunning variety of signifiers – from living creatures to inanimate objects, from organic beings to inorganic objects, from the material to the abstract. These 'movements,' coming from an excess of phenomena, were the minimal units constituting the work.

Combinations of 'Movements'

What Hijikata sought most through serial performances for Hakutōbō was to continuously develop or create new 'movements,' rather to release new works. In making *Costume en Face*, Hijikata prepared 337 'movements' for Yamamoto and composed the work by combining them. Those 337 'movements' are the minimal units making up the work, and these minimal units were connected to each other as if spun to create longer sequences of 'movements,' which were in turn used to compose scenes and then integrated into a complete work.

The process of direction – how to arrange the 'movements' in a work, how to combine them, and how to connect or bridge 'movements' – was non-linear and contingent. There are innumerable 'movement' combinations and how to bridge them was affected by various conditions. Decisions of structure could be either inevitable or accidental. The composition process was characterized by great complexity.

Were 'movements' stored in a manner such that they were connected by images and occurred in succession? Or were they classified systematically based on some sort of criteria? We know nothing at all about the form of the 'movement' archive in Hijikata's brain, but we can glean something of the composition process from the notebook notation transcribed by Moe Yamamoto.

We can only say that 'movements' described in the notation were selected taking into consideration various conditions to complete the performance, including the dancer's attributes and technical level, the world of the work containing its theme and motif, as well as specific pieces of art and music that informed the world of the dance, and then all these were composed into a work and combined in scenes. This trial process was repeated. The provisional flow of these scenes is represented in this notebook notation. Once 'movements' were decided and transcribed, they were bestowed with time, occupied space, and reacted to lighting, art and music – giving form to the work.

Archive of 'Movements'

This publication of the notebook notation of *Costume en Face* is meant to provide partial material in order to consider the structure and methodology of Hijikata's Butoh, and particularly his use of notation in both the immediate process of composition and as a more distant resource for movement. This publication – itself written in a way that is opaque to easy understanding – is only one piece of the puzzle, however. In addition to the notebook notation, there is a film of the original performance, as well as a scrapbook of images created by Hijikata as source material for the creation of movement. Finally, the original performers of these works, who are still living, are an incredible resource to help bring the movements named here back to the body.

At the Hijikata Archive, we began a project some years ago that we called The Archive of Movement. In it, we asked Moe Yamamoto to recreate as many of the 337 'movements' notated in the notebook, and recorded each 'movement' on camera. We have done this also with Yukio Waguri and his many 'movements,' so that the total number of named 'movements' that have been documented in their physicalized form number over 1500. By recording in film the 'movements' of *Butoh-fū*, we hope to reveal the structure of Hijikata's notational Butoh. And while the 'movements,' in isolation, lack the meaning that they carried when situated by Hijikata within a total work, it is also possible that contemporary dancers and choreographers might make use of the imagery and methodology embedded in Hijikata's *Butoh-fū*.

NOTES

1. Interview with Moe Yamamoto by Takashi Morishita on May 25, 2007, when the *Costume en Face* video was screened at Raiosha, Hiyoshi Campus, Keio University.
2. Nevertheless, there were not necessarily messages in the words provided by Hijikata to the dancers. The words both denoted and connoted semiotically. But without understanding Hijikata's unique codes, even efforts to create a collection of Hijikata's Butoh cannot ultimately be valid.
3. The names of scenes were not originally given, but the words/phrases were written down in relevant places in the notes. As for a., b., and c., however, there are seen no names and the author gave them on his own responsibility. In "Psychology," the ending scene is deemed to also be psychology; therefore there are two "psychology" scenes.
4. *"Shinrabanshō wo Kanjitoru Gokui"* ["The Secrets to Sensing All Things in the Natural Universe"], in the monthly art magazine *Geijutsu Seikatsu* [*Art Life*], January 1978.
5. Yamamoto himself said his dancing (in *Costume en Face*) was less intense than Yoko Ashikawa's, citing his own immature technique.

EDITOR'S NOTE

This project began five years ago, when I read excerpts from Hijikata's essays in a crucial issue of *The Drama Review* dedicated to his work ("Tatsumi Hijikata and The Words of Butoh," Spring 2000, Vol. 44, No.1). His striking language and imagery built and dismantled bodies, transgressing divisions between the human, social, spirit and animal worlds. His language danced indelibly. When I approached Takashi Morishita, the director of the Hijikata Archive at Keio University Art Center, to see if we might translate one of his many unpublished writings for Ugly Duckling Presse, he directed my attention to the amazing notebook notations through which Hijikata both composed and notated movements, sequences, and scenes for particular works. Not only had these remained untranslated, they had never been published even in Japanese.

We are enormously excited to finally publish *Costume en Face* as the fourth book in our Emergency Playscripts series, a project that takes up the challenge of publishing performance texts that lie outside conventional acts of notation. In the case of *Costume en Face*, this took enormous effort by Sawako Nakayasu, who translated the text, and Steven Chodoriwsky, who designed the book, since both strove to create a work that was both readable and at the same time true to the provisional, dynamic state of the notebook from which they began. Nor could this project have happened without the support and generosity of the Hijikata Archive's Takashi Morishita and Yu Homma, Keio University's Professor Hayato Kosuge, and of course Moe Yamamoto himself.

Though I hope that this book will open avenues of scholarship about Hijikata's Butoh, I have even greater hopes that it will inspire contemporary artists and choreographers to approach Butoh, and notation, with increased vigor. Perhaps, also, it might encourage other attempts at translating the mountain of Hijikata's difficult but important writings, which now lay dark and inaccessible to so many of us.

YELENA GLUZMAN
UNIVERSITY OF CALIFORNIA, SAN DIEGO

INDEX

Allah, 84-85, 90-91
Amamiya [first name Ikko; a dancer], 54-55, 104, 106
Ariadne, 26, 28, 32-33, 76-77
Asa [possibly an abbrev. of Asada], 116, 118
Asada [first name Tetsuya; a dancer], 84-85, 104, 106, 117, 119

Bacon, Francis, 46-47, 84-85, 102-03
Beardsley, Aubrey, 30-31, 56-57, 80, 82, 104, 106, 108-9, 112-13
Beardsley, Madame [probably a character from Beardsley], 26, 28, 32-33
Bellmer, Hans, 26, 28, 50-51
Boccaccio, Madame [probably a character from Boccaccio], 76, 77, 80, 82
Buddha, 27, 29

Dali, Salvador, 80-83
Da Vinci, Leonardo, 26, 28, 88-89
Dubuffet, Jean, 50-51
Delaunay, Robert, 32-33, 80-83, 108-11

Ebisu [god of fisherman & merchants], 44-45

Fautrier, Jean, 27, 29, 32-33, 38-39, 72-73, 80-83, 92-95, 98-99, 110-13
Fuji [possibly an abbrev. of Fujino], 86-87
Fujino [a dancer; also referred to by first name, Seizō], 116-19

gabu [Noh mask], 72-73, 117, 119
Gaki [hungry ghost], 16-19
geisha, 78-79
Gigaku mask [used in the ancient dance form Gigaku], 22, 24, 76-77, 98-99, 108-11, 123, 125
Gōchoku [family name Matsumoto; a dancer], 116-19
Goya, Francisco, 22, 24, 26, 28, 34, 36, 38-9, 46-47, 56-57, 80-83, 88-89, 94-95, 98-99, 117, 119

Hachiman Taro [Japanese commander], 50-51
Hyakki Yagyō [night parade of one hundred demons], 16-17, 22, 24, 27, 29, 72-73, 108-9, 123, 125
Hanako [...], 63, 65, 108-9
Hotei [god of abundance & happiness], 40-41, 44-45

Kaguya [female character from folklore], 46-47
Kannon [goddess], 72-73,
Kiyohime [snake princess], 100-1
Koharu [*geisha* song], 46-47, 78-79
Kotarō [...], 18-19
Koyama [...], 66, 84-87, 104, 106

Maikubi [entity of dancing heads], 16-19, 22-25, 108-9, 123, 125
menko [card-slapping game], 46-47, 78-79

Mon [family name Kumagai; a dancer], 116-121

nikawa [glue made from cowhide], 116, 118, 120-21
Nishimura [...], 80, 82
Nopperabō [faceless ghost], 28-29

Ōigawa [peeping tom], 35, 37
Okame [ugly, good-natured woman], 22, 24, 108-9, 110-11
Orpheus, 30-31, 72-73, 112-13
Oshira-sama [god of silkwoms & agriculture], 32-33

Peacock, Madame [...], 26-29, 76-77
Picasso, Pablo, 30-31, 72-73, 98-99

Redon, Odilon, 22, 24, 30-31, 80, 82

Seizō, see Fujino
Sekido [first name Tomohiro; a dancer], 56-57
shōgi [Japanese chess], 72-73
Solomon, 84-85, 102-3, 116, 118
Sonnenstern, Friedrich Schröder [also abbrev. as Sonnen], 32-33, 84-85

tabi [socks], 120-21
Tanaka [...], 38-39
tarako [cod roe], 30-31, 40-41, 108-9
Tengu [long-nosed goblin], 22-25, 27, 29, 108-11
tokiwa [unchanging stones], 36-37
Toyen (Marie Čermínová), 26-29, 32-33, 98-99, 112-13
Tristan, 54-55, 110-11

Umibōzu [ocean ghost], 26, 28

Waguri [first name Yukio; a dancer], 86-87, 104, 106
Wols (Alfred Otto Wolfgang Schulze), 30-31

yajirobē [balancing toy], 72-73
Yakubyōgami [god of pestilence], 16-17, 22-25
Yamamoto [first name Moe; lead dancer], 11, 22, 24, 30-31, 71, 86-87, 104, 106, 114-116, 118, 127
Yokota [first name Kazunobu; a dancer], 34, 36, 84-85

COSTUME EN FACE: A PRIMER OF DARKNESS FOR YOUNG BOYS AND GIRLS

This second printing of six hundred copies was printed and bound in April 2018 by MᶜNAUGHTON & GUNN in Saline, Michigan, using 100% recycled paper. The cover was printed offset by PRESTIGE PRINTING in Brooklyn, New York on a FRENCH PAPER COMPANY cover stock. One thousand and two hundred copies of the first printing were made in January 2015.

Initial transcription of Moe Yamamoto's notebook to digital file by Mutsumi Horning. Design by Steven Chodoriwsky. Typeset in Akzidenz Grotesk, Hiragino Kaku Gothic, and Orator. EMERGENCY PLAYSCRIPTS series design by DON'T LOOK NOW!

Funding for this edition was provided in part by Keio University Art Center, the Foundation for Contemporary Arts, and the National Endowment for the Arts.

EMERGENCY PLAYSCRIPTS promotes texts which, through their performance, can expand the practice of theater. The series is edited by Yelena Gluzman and published by Auguste & Louis Lumière for UGLY DUCKLING PRESSE.

EMERGENCY PLAYSCRIPTS:

HELLO FAILURE by Kristen Kosmas
(2009)

CONCERTOS by No Collective
(2011)

NOT KNOWING by Mike Taylor
(2014)

COSTUME EN FACE by Tatsumi Hijikata
(2015)

A PIECE OF WORK by Annie Dorsen
(2017)